BRONWYN DAVIDS

Lansdowne Dearest

My family's story of forced removals

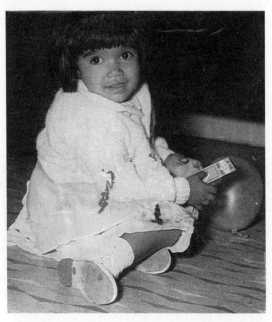

Dressed up for a double wedding in Goedverwacht, 1964.

KWELA BOOKS

Kwela Books,
an imprint of NB Publishers, a division of Media24 Boeke (Pty) Ltd
40 Heerengracht, Cape Town, South Africa
PO Box 879, Cape Town 8000, South Africa
www.kwela.com

Cover design: Wilna Combrinck
Cover image: Bronwyn's second birthday party, 1963
Typography: Nazli Jacobs
Editor: Karin Schimke
Proof reader: Glynne Newlands
Set in Nimrod

Printed by **novus print**, a division of Novus Holdings

First published by Kwela Books 2020

ISBN: 978-0-7957-0980-7
ISBN: 978-0-7957-0981-4 (epub)
ISBN: 978-0-7957-0982-1 (mobi)

Dedicated to kind people,
wherever you may find yourself in the world

Maternal line

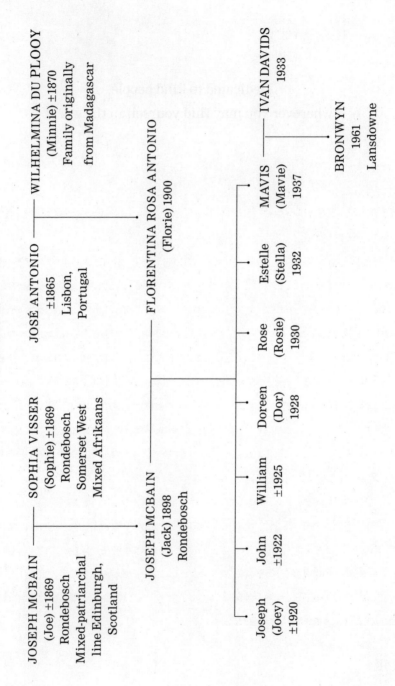

JOSEPH MCBAIN (Joe) ±1869 Rondebosch Mixed-patriarchal line Edinburgh, Scotland — SOPHIA VISSER (Sophie) ±1869 Rondebosch Somerset West Mixed Afrikaans

JOSÉ ANTONIO ±1865 Lisbon, Portugal — WILHELMINA DU PLOOY (Minnie) ±1870 Family originally from Madagascar

JOSEPH MCBAIN (Jack) 1898 Rondebosch — FLORENTINA ROSA ANTONIO (Florie) 1900

Joseph (Joey) ±1920

John ±1922

William ±1925

Doreen (Dor) 1928

Rose (Rosie) 1930

Estelle (Stella) 1932

MAVIS (Mavie) 1937 — IVAN DAVIDS 1933

BRONWYN 1961 Lansdowne

Author's note

IF YOU SEE the past in terms of numbers, it becomes a lot easier to understand.

In the present, there is one singular I. Before that there were two parents, four grandparents, eight great-grandparents, sixteen great-great-grandparents, and so on. The story that follows is minute in scale to the stories that could have been told of this ray of ancestry reaching back, right out and far away from Africa.

Please note that some dates used in the first chapter are estimates, like the exact date Great-grandpa Joe bought the family property, and when and where my uncles were born. Also, to avoid confusion, I have called my parents by their names, Mavie and Ivan, and so too the two aunts we lived with.

The titles of the opening and closing chapters are taken from The Confiteor, a prayer said at the start of the Catholic mass. These lines are from the start of the prayer: 'I confess to almighty God and to you, my brothers and sisters . . . that I have greatly sinned *in my thoughts and in my words,* in what I have done and what I have failed to do.'

Contents

DRAWING OF THE MCBAIN PROPERTY

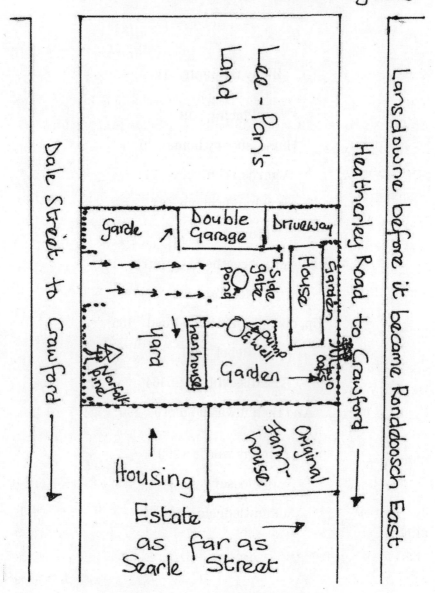

Lansdowne Road to Claremont

to Lower Lansdowne & Railway Line

Lee-Pan's Land

Dale Street to Crawford

Heatherley Road to Crawford

Lansdowne before it became Ronddoosch East

Garde

Double Garage

Driveway

Garden

House

Side gate

Pond

Yard

henhouse

pump & well

Garden

Norfolk Pine

Original Farm-house

Housing Estate as far as Searle Street

In my thoughts

A LONG TIME AGO I used to have another life, very different from the one that I have now. I used to have people I could go to. And they provided a sense of home, generosity and warmth that I am unlikely to find again in this city or anywhere else in the world, come to think of it.

Sometimes I take a trip down memory lane to revisit that life.

I travel by train on the Cape Flats line to Lansdowne Station and take my time walking up Lansdowne Road. I stop off at Shoprite and at Half Price Store to buy colourful balls of yarn for the little girl whose mom I am going to visit.

I pop in at Queen Bess Store and look in at the windows of Mrs Israel's mishmash of a store. I spend a long time at the Book Swop Shop. Then I stop off at the surgery on the corner of Hanbury Avenue to greet Dor through the dispensary window. Finally, I cross over to the field at bus stop 12 and into Dale Street, to enter the family property via the long, wide backyard driveway.

If I'd come by bus from Claremont, I would have disembarked at bus stop 11 and walked down Lansdowne Road, again stopping off at all the quaint shops: Hamid's, chock-full of all kinds of everything, Tobias Clothing and Haberdashers, then over the road to see what was playing at The Broadway Bioscope, cross back over to Niefies to check out their British magazines, then back to Lee-Pan's shop where there are more interesting goods to marvel at – the soft, textured paper, the fountain pens and the different colour inks.

Before the walkabout, I always buy plain Simba or Messaris Chilli chips to munch on, and a Groovy Grapefruit or a Double 'O' drink. It's thirsty and hungry work absorbing the details and images of a place where life was bipolar.

It's not far to walk down Heatherley Road to reach the side gate to the property. I crunch along the grey gravel aggregate driveway, careful not to get the loose stones in my shoes, past a riot of hedges and creepers on my left. Sometimes I can't resist climbing up the mound of ochre-coloured gravel – my great-grandfather's unfinished ideas – impacted hard over decades, before the wooden shuttered window on that side of the house.

On the right side of the driveway, which has parking space for at least four cars, sandstone rocks are placed along the zinc fence draped with morning glory. At the end of the driveway is a pitch-roof garage with barn-style doors, tall enough for a lorry to pass through easily.

Linking the garage to the house is a three-metre-high court-yard wall, originally constructed with grey stone blocks. The walls are covered with lichen, with flashes of bright green moss in the crevices.

I have to jiggle the latch to open the weathered grey shed gate with letterbox number 10. The gate could do with a lick of varnish.

Through the wooden gate, I'm greeted with a cheery 'Hello, Pretty!' from the red-plumed parrot Polly. The parrot's cage is perched on a sandstone rockery, out of which a metres-high Queen of the Night cactus grows. It blooms once a year in the moonlight from dusk to dawn, an event my aunt's husband likes to record by taking time-lapse photos.

Visits to Lansdowne never fail to provide a feast for the senses, mostly visual. I long to be able to draw or photograph what I see, to capture the many fleeting impressions that change with the seasons.

As soon as I step through that gate, the children stop their games and crowd around me to bombard me with questions or to regale me with far-fetched tales. I know all their names and their odd quirks of character and their even odder turns of phrase.

Whenever I hear the Joan Baez song 'Children and all that jazz', which is not often these days, I think of those kids. They don't live at this house – they only came to play. It is the kind of place and time when children play outdoors all day long, quibbling over the rules of the games and often making up their own as they go along.

And they cross-question unsuspecting visitors about why they've been gone so long.

'I went far away,' I tell them.

'Why? Did you go to England? We know lots of aunties who go to England!'

I grin at them. 'I went away to learn how to listen to people. So that I could write a book.'

'What book? One with pictures, like *Peter Pan*?'

'You *bis*,' I say, laughing. *Bis* their word for 'busybody', used when someone asks too many questions.

I tug a few plaits and tickle some stick-people necks. 'I went away so that I could learn to write an epitaph for a time and a place that no longer exists.'

'Ohhh!' they say, in unison. And just like that, they jostle each other to get back to their game, no longer heeding me as I make my way to the always-open grey stable kitchen door.

'Hello, stranger!' Mavie says, all smiles. 'Long time no see! Come in. Sit. Sit, and we'll have some tea while we chat. There's still chocolate cake from the weekend.'

She's excited, as she always is, at the prospect of sharing a good yarn or two. 'Look at you, burnt to a crisp! And look how long your hair has grown! How was it, over there? How was Spain? How was Portugal?'

Mavie and the house at 10 Heatherley Road is exactly what it is in these journeys: home. My home in Lansdowne, a suburb about ten kilometres southeast of central Cape Town.

At times when the kitchen would be particularly busy, usually with cooking and baking, I would wait out the storm in the sprawling garden, breathing in the fragrances from the fruit trees and luxuriating in the cool shade. Some days I would swing in the swing tied to a branch of the 40-year-old oak tree and dream.

On these trips down memory lane, I go to see how things had turned out for Mavie and family.

Not well, I'm afraid. So much loss and sadness. 'Home' was situated in the time of apartheid's forced removals. There were moves afoot that would drastically alter the lives of hundreds of thousands of people, including my family, the one at Heatherley Road. All these people had the same uncertainty in common. What now? Where to next?

In the 1960s, throughout the city, there was a funereal pall, coupled with a pervasive atmosphere of shame and sadness. There was anger and disappointment at being unfairly treated, humiliated, disrespected, betrayed. All wrapped in a mantle of anxiety, insecurity and tension.

The winds of change blowing through the African continent, that British Prime Minister Harold Macmillan warned the South African government about in February 1960, were gathering momentum. But instead of bringing freedom to South Africans, the wind created disruption and chaos on an unprecedented scale. It would soon reach hurricane status. It lasted for decades, and to this day, the toll is still being counted on the violence-torn Cape Flats.

This is the story of what happened to my family and to me and to everyone we knew during those dark and tumultuous years when whole communities and entire ways of living were lost.

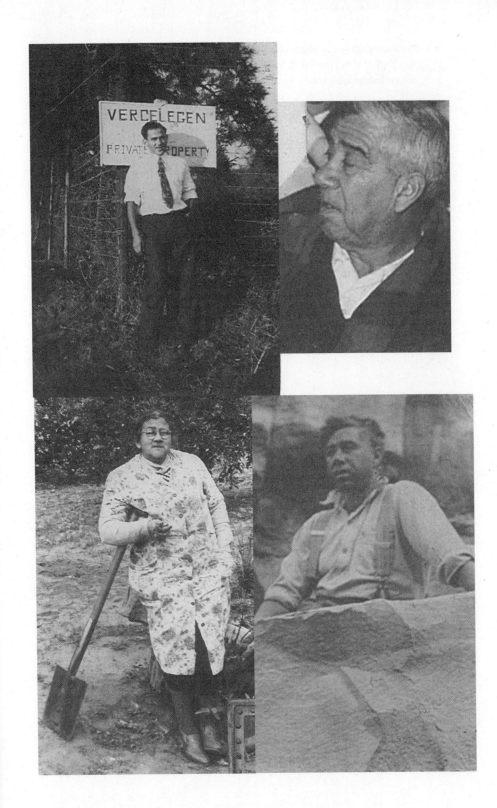

Previous page, anti-clockwise:
Jose and Minnie Antonio in 1903 with three-year-old Florie beside her mother and cousin Anne.

A young Joey on Chapman's Peak.

Florentina Antonio in 1913 on her Confirmation day.

Grandma Florie gardening in Goedverwacht, 1962.

A pensive Grandpa Jack, 1950s.

Grandpa Jack, 1963.

A young William outside the wine farm, Vergelegen in Somerset West. Some of Sophie Visser McBain's family worked and lived here.

Placing

IN THE BEGINNING, there was fertile land. Soon there was a house. A garden grew. And a family lived there whose certainties over time were buffeted by changes that nobody could have foreseen.

This family's story began one morning in August 1920 when Joseph McBain from Albion Road, Rondebosch saw a property-for-sale advert in the *Cape Times*.

At 50-something Joe, as everyone called him, looked at his new-born grandson Joey and read him the advert. There were raised eyebrows, smirks and averted eyes from his wife Sophie – an Afrikaans-speaking coloured woman from the Visser family in Somerset West – his only son Jack and his nervous wreck of a niece Dolly. His twenty-year-old daughter-in-law Florie had eyes only for her Joey, resting in her arms.

'What do you think, my boy?' Joe asked baby Joey. 'Must I take the savings and buy us some land, where you can run and play? And we can grow our own fruit and veg and have chickens and Muskovies and a dog. Just think of it, eh?'

Green-eyed Joey yawned. He was a baby on a mission to have some peace and quiet, but he took the time to give the tall talking shape a blessing of dribble.

With his grandson in mind, Joe walked into the Cape-to-Cairo Building in central Cape Town a few days later. Around him were a Chinese man, an Englishman, an Indian and several born-and-bred Capetonians, all wanting to have a look at the map of plots for sale in Lansdowne.

With his brutally forthright wife Sophie's words still ringing in his ears, Joe eagerly scanned the map. *'Is jy mal in jou kop, ou man?'* Sophie scolded, tapping her temple with a finger to show just how mad she thought her old man was. 'We're happy here in Rondebosch. Hoekom moet jy alles bederf?'

Joe chuckled. Sophie's rages always spurred him on to strive harder to improve their living conditions – to do better and to be a worthier person.

Joe's grandfather had been one of three brothers from Edinburgh, Scotland, who got off the boat in Table Bay Harbour some time in the 1820s. They settled down in Cape Town, started small businesses and eventually married local women. A fourth brother settled in Port Elizabeth.

At the estate agency in the Cape-to-Cairo Building, the Englishman bought plots 11 and 13 Heatherley Road. An Indian man bought the plot on the corner of Lansdowne and Wurzberg Avenue. A Chinese started at Lansdowne Road and bought plots as far as number 8 Heatherley Road. On the Dale Street side of the block, his purchase stopped at number 3.

Joe chose numbers 10 and 12 Heatherley Road and numbers 5, 7 and 9 Dale Street. Altogether about 2 000 square metres. For a brief moment, he thought of buying the land as far as Searle Street, which ran alongside a small vlei. But the farmer whose land was being parcelled off for the newly rezoned residential area of Heatherley Estate still lived at his house at number 14. Joe wanted his plots to be all together.

Besides that, hastily made sums in his head revealed that bond payments would be far greater than the £1.10 he was able to afford a month. Better to be safe than sorry, he thought. In the building trade, where he was a bricklayer with a side-line cartage business, things could change in an instant. This made him reminisce about some of the buildings he'd worked on. Like the rugby stadium at Newlands – a grand project, something to be proud of, even if his favourite games had always been soccer and cricket.

His son Jack had his trade as a coachworks upholsterer, but who knew what the future held? Joe was optimistic but also cautious. There had been some harsh years.

There was the Great War, one of the bloodiest conflicts in human history, which led directly to the deaths of nine million combatants and seven million civilians. Indirectly, World War I led to the Spanish flu pandemic of 1918 spread by soldiers returning after the war. An estimated 500 million people were infected globally. Joe McBain's sister Laurie was one of 50 million people who died of the flu.

The loss of his dear youngest sister cut like a knife. He and Sophie undertook to look after her orphaned daughter Dolly, a rather frail girl who had just finished school and worked at a dressmaker's boutique in Claremont.

Although Sophie was a hard nut to crack, she was praised by many for her generosity and willingness to take care of people, either providing food parcels or taking in waifs and strays. Joe's brother gave Sophie a wide berth after he ended up on the wrong side of her for something quite small. At least his sister Maggie, who lived in a cottage beside the railway line in Wilderness Road, Claremont, still visited and so did his sister Annie.

When Joe's son Jack married Florie in 1919, Joe could see his family expanding. Florie was a nice young woman with a family background that fascinated him: her father, José Antonio, hailed from Lisbon, Portugal.

In the 1890s, after a few rough months at sea, José and some of his shipmates jumped ship in Table Bay Harbour. The houses that were piled up on the lower slopes of the mountain reminded them a bit of home, and he decided to stay. José Antonio lived in the Loader Street area in Green Point, finding board with a local family, while his friends made their way to the fishermen's community of Kalk Bay.

José befriended his neighbours, who were descended from Madagascan creoles who had somehow found their way on to a ship to Cape Town. He knew some French and they knew some Portuguese and they added in English bit by bit as their proficiency in the language grew. English, of course, was a necessity for life in Cape Town.

After several odd jobs, José eventually found work as a gardener at Sans Souci Estate in Newlands. He was then able to marry Minnie Du Plooy, the Madagascan neighbour's sister, at St Mary's Cathedral in Roeland Street, Cape Town[1].

---

1   After consultation with two of the grandchildren of great-grandma Minnie's brothers, I learnt that her family was English-speaking, except for her brother William, who married a white Afrikaans woman from Saron. We came to the conclusion that their original Madagascan surname was not understood when they registered on arrival in Cape Town and they were therefore recorded with the more familiar Cape French Huguenot surname of Du Plooy. This happened to many foreigners who arrived in the late 1800s. Portuguese surnames were also phonetically translated into English, as was the case with the Portuguese husbands of two of great-grandma Minnie's nieces.

José attended mass at St Mary's and belonged to the Knights of Da Gama Society, a Portuguese men's church group. For church feast days he would dress up in his Sunday best and wear the Society's sash and participate in the processions around the streets of Cape Town, starting at Hope Street and going into Roeland Street.

Minnie continued to work in service at an estate house in Newlands but, once their only child Florentina Rosa was born in 1900, she stayed home. Florie, as she would be called, attended the majority white convent school at St Michael's in Rondebosch although she was of mixed heritage. Many immigrants sent their children there to be educated.

Due to his own heritage of being a Euro-Cape slave mixture, Joe became the glue that held the McBain and Antonio families together. He came from an English language background, with the usual smattering of made-in-Cape-Town Afrikaans.

Joe's son Jack and José's daughter Florie married at St Michael's in Rondebosch, and it was decided that their children would be brought up Catholic, instead of joining St Paul's Anglican Church, to which Joe's family belonged. Although at least three generations of McBains had been baptised into St Paul's, Joe didn't mind the line being broken. He had, after all, married Sophie, who'd been raised Methodist in Somerset West. She'd converted to the Anglican tradition when she married Joe.

Jack was their only child, and he'd been indulged. He was scatterbrained but full of strong opinions. His offspring, for instance, was to speak English. He prided himself on having attended Battswood. Many of his classmates had gone on to study to be teachers[2]. In those years, the much-respected Teacher Training Colleges of Cape Town emphasised discipline, decency, being attentive and obedient, a good work ethic and a willingness to learn. Those were the qualities Jack admired and wanted for his family, starting with Joey the charmer.

As Joe McBain stood in the property development agency in Cape Town that morning some time around 1920, he visualised a better life for all of them: his wife Sophie, his niece Dolly, his son Jack, his daughter-in-law Florie and the baby grandson Joey, who'd been named for him. He imagined a place where there would be space to grow.

When Joe got home, Sophie was still *dikbek* about his intention to buy land so he celebrated his purchases silently with two helpings of tomato bredie and rice and an extra big helping of bread-and-butter pudding, finishing off with his beer stein filled with *moerkoffie*.

---

2   Battswood School was established in 1891 by Martha Grey, the 8th Countess of Stamford. She was born as Martha Solomons from a slave mother in 1838, at the time of the abolishment of slavery in the Cape. She met Reverend Harry Grey, an ordained Anglican clergyman from Cheshire, England in 1864 when he was working as a labourer in the Wellington area. Grey, cousin to the 7th Earl of Stamford, was sent to South Africa on remittance by his family because of his hard-drinking habit. When the Earl of Stamford died in 1883 without leaving an heir, Reverend Grey inherited the title and the family estate at Dunham Massey.
   Harry and Martha entered into a relationship in 1874. They had their first son, John, in 1879 and a daughter, Frances, soon after. They married in 1880 and settled in Wynberg. A third child, Mary, was born in 1882. Until his death in 1890 Harry never returned to England to live there. He left his family, who had always been marginalised by the English society in Cape Town, quite well off. That afforded Martha, Countess of Stamford, the opportunity to establish educational facilities for coloured children descended from 186 years of slavery at the Cape.
   Wikipedia contributors. 3 June 2017. *Martha Grey, Countess of Stamford*. Wikipedia, The Free Encyclopedia. https://en.wikipedia.org/w/index.php?title=Martha_Grey,_Countess_of_Stamford&oldid=783622322. Last accessed 03/03/2020.

24

In time they will come around, he thought as he settled down after supper to read from the American Bible Society's Centenary Bible[3], which he'd bought for himself on the Grand Parade. It was a big edition with cream-coloured pages and he enjoyed poring over the many illustrations, especially the ones of the plants and fruit trees of the Holy Land.

He'd browse through Proverbs and chuckle to himself when he read in chapter 27, verses 15–16: 'A nagging wife is like the dripping of a leaky roof in a rainstorm. Stopping her is like trying to stop the wind. It's like trying to grab olive oil with your hand.'

He looked over at Sophie, who was strumming her 16-string lyre to get Joey in his crib off to sleep. Her playing and singing were good. She had sung in the choir in her young days at the Methodist Church.

'*Wat? Wat loer jy*?' she snapped, catching him watching her.

He smiled at her and flipped the page back. And nearly dropped the heavy Bible when he read in Proverbs 19:13. 'A foolish son is ruin to his father, and a wife's quarrelling is a continual dripping of rain.' They lived in the right place for that, he thought, because the Newlands area always has the highest rainfall in the Cape, or so the newspaper said.

The next day he walked from Rondebosch to Lansdowne and breathed in lungs full of fresh air. At the new plots, he dug his hands into the black soil to feel the texture. There was moisture in that soil. This pleased him. He imagined his garden as he stood there surveying the land which would soon be his, once the bond approval and deeds of sale came through.

---

3   During my research for this book, I googled that particular Bible and found a second-hand copy being advertised for $699.

This was going to be a good place for his family, he thought.

On his walk back home, he didn't take the back roads but went along the main roads until he reached Sans Souci Estate in Newlands. There he found his daughter-in-law's father José Antonio picking ripe persimmons from a heavily laden tree and placing them in baskets to be taken to the kitchen.

He told José Antonio what he had done. 'I will help build *casa e jardim, amigo,*' his Portuguese friend told him.

They shook hands to seal the deal. Joe was pleased.

'Now we go to my *casa*, time for *café e pasteis de nata,*' José beamed at him, using the Portuguese term for Minnie's melktert.

He led the way to the tiny cottage where they lived, in a row of houses that bordered onto the estate's grounds.

A few months later with plans in hand, Joe and Jack, José Antonio and a few of Sophie's brothers and brothers-in-law from Somerset West set about clearing the land. Soon they were laying the foundations and then slowly they began to build a house that could easily be expanded over time.

An outhouse was built on the 9 Dale Street boundary. At the point where all four plots met, a deep well was dug and lined with concrete and bricks. They built a garage for tools and the storage of building materials at 10 Heatherley Road. They marked off where the house would start at number 10, inching a little bit over onto number 12.

Soon the walls were rising on two master bedrooms on either side of a long, wide passage. These were supplemented by a smaller bedroom, a living room, a kitchen and a bathroom. In front of the house was a wide veranda enclosed with windows. Joe included long concrete shelves on either side of the entrance below the windows as he intended using the veranda as a greenhouse for his seedlings.

When the extended family – Joe, Sophie, Jack, Florie, baby Joey and Cousin Dolly – moved to their new home, Lansdowne Road was still a dirt track, but everywhere around them, people were building new houses. With the help of José Antonio, the garden was established, soon delivering healthy crops and fruit to feed the family and anyone who came to visit.

Throughout the 1920s, Jack's family grew steadily with the arrival of John and William. By the time Doreen was born in 1928, Joe McBain's cartage company was doing well enough, especially with country area contracts. This was when work was scarce, just after the Wall Street Crash of 1929 which led to the Great Depression.

It was a time of great deprivation and hardship. Jack had been in the automobile-coachworks industry and lost his job during the Depression. He was forced to join builder crews that often worked on sites in other provinces, such as Nelspruit in the Transvaal. On his return home he became restless and morose. Soon after his fifth child Rose was born in 1930, he started an affair with Lizzie, a woman from Black River and a good friend of cousin Dolly.

It took only eleven years to sour the safe, secure and rather idyllic home life Joe wanted to create for his family. Jack's infidelity with Lizzie lasted for decades and led to extreme levels of stress and tension in the house.

Joe remained optimistic in spite of his difficult son Jack. He extended the living room and the kitchen and built a fourth bedroom, expanded the bathroom, toilet and pantry, all of similar dimensions, namely 4 x 3 metres.

He closed off the veranda area for rooms for the three boys and Sophie's nephews from Somerset West, and even friends of friends who needed a place to stay for a while. They found refuge there until they could establish themselves in the city.

Jack was always away, courting his goose. Joe was disappointed in his son, but he dared not voice this to Sophie, who would have ripped out his guts for extra-extra-large garters.

When things got too much, Joe walked to Kirstenbosch Gardens and climbed up Skeleton Gorge. He often saw General Jan Smuts up on Table Mountain – many mountaineers of the day could attest to be on greeting terms with then Prime Minister of South Africa.

In 1932, Stella was born, Jack and Florie's sixth child and third daughter. Five years later, on New Year's Day 1937, Mavie followed, bringing the family to seven children. Jack continued his affair with his mistress, whose jealousy he pacified by claiming that Mavie was not his child. He lied and said that his wife had, in fact, cheated on him with an Indian. After all, look how much darker the child was compared to the other girls!

He distanced himself from the baby and when Mavie grew into a toddler, he was often deliberately spiteful and hurtful by pushing her out of the way. In time, she placed her trust only in her mother and her sisters. Her grandfathers and her brothers became her many fathers.

Florie was a nervous wreck and, what with her husband's atrocious behaviour and seven children to look after, she aged faster than was necessary. After finishing the household chores at Heatherley Road she spent much of her time with her parents José and Minnie, who by then had moved to a cottage in Chichester Road, Claremont, a twenty-minute walk away.

Florie fretted about what would happen to her and her girls when her father-in-law wasn't around anymore. Where would they go? How would they live? The boys were in their teens already and would soon be able to carve out their own lives.

The Great Depression of the 1930s flowed into World War II. It was a time of scarcity and fear, but people remained hospitable. They did not close themselves off. They adopted an attitude of 'just because things are bad, doesn't mean we must drop our standards'.

Florie endured two big knocks in a row. In Claremont, her mom Minnie died after a short illness. A few months later she learnt her husband's mistress Lizzie had given birth to baby Kenneth, Jack's fourth son.

Over time, Florie and Kenny would become good friends. They first bonded when he was ten years old. Jack brought him along one day and left him in the car in the yard while he came in to have lunch. Seeing the boy, Florie insisted that he join them at the table. Kenny became part of the family's life. He grew up to be a kind man, a person of principle and ethics, independent of his parents' lifestyle. Kenny always said that he did not know that his father never stayed with them. When he was little, Jack would be there in the morning and he would be there when he went to sleep at night. It was only from the time that he was taken to Heatherley Road that he realised things were not what they had seemed to him.

But all those years before that, without the benefit of hindsight, it was hard for Florie to hide her misery from her children, especially the younger ones who had not yet started school. They were always around to witness Florie calling Jack out into the yard to give voice to her many grievances, including failure to provide money for food and clothing for the children.

All Jack's money went to supporting his second family and

Joe had to keep everyone fed and clothed. Sophie had never been an easy person to live with, and that was another matter that Florie had to grapple with daily. She loved her mother-in-law's Somerset West family, though, and always kept in contact with them.

Florie was grateful that she could find solace in her religion. Being scorned, enduring mockery, humiliation and hurt, strengthened her faith. She and the girls could also seek refuge during the day at her father's new home in Lawson Road just down Heatherley Road, in a granny cottage with a separate entrance. They would walk along a narrow pathway past the small lakes, marvelling at how every vlei was being filled in with rubble. They watched the roads being extended and houses being built. And eventually they met the people who moved into their new homes, happy and full of optimism.

As the war progressed, a family friend who was in the Royal Air Force wanted to take Florie's oldest son Joey with him to England to join the RAF. Joe and Sophie flatly refused to let him go. Florie recognised it as an opportunity, but she didn't want to see her boy go to war either.

Around that time José Antonio became ill and Florie nursed him. He died just before the end of the war.

The loss of her father renewed Florie's fears. She thought that without him there, she would surely be facing divorce and homelessness. Her anxiety about where to go with her girls knew no bounds. Fear of ending up in the gutter played on her mind. But her greatest fear was losing her place in church and being denied communion if she was divorced. It was considered a sin for a Catholic to be divorced and it meant you could not receive communion, nor could you remarry in the church. To this day, there are Catholics who will tough out an unpleasant marriage rather than get divorced.

Joe assured her that she and her daughters could stay and that there would be no divorce from Jack in his lifetime. He kept peace with his son too by going along with Sophie to meet Lizzie and her family.

The old man had always been more of a father to his grandchildren than Jack and they worshipped him for it. He taught them how to build and garden and fix things. Some days he'd walk all his grandchildren and their friends to the Youngsfield airstrip, which was busy during and immediately after the war years, to watch the planes come and go.

Some days he would just sit outside the kitchen door on a wicker chair, smoking his tobacco pipe, reading the *Cape Times* in the morning and the *Cape Argus* in the afternoon and drinking coffee, waiting for visitors. Somebody would always pop in for a chat eventually.

Hospitality was important to Joe and his family. 'Be not forgetful to entertain strangers: for thereby some have entertained angels unawares.' Hebrews 12, verse 12. When he bought his big Bible, which was kept on the sideboard in the lounge, it was one of the first verses he paged to and read aloud to himself.

He missed his Portuguese *amigo*. The fruit trees and the vegetable patch delivered bounty after bounty. Whatever the season, the McBains had plenty, a blessing with so many mouths to feed.

When Joe sat outside like that, the pergola overhead hanging heavy with bunches of grapes, he would become nostalgic for the times he and the grandchildren would take the train from Claremont to Kalk Bay with José Antonio to visit the Portuguese friends José had arrived in Cape Town with. They had done well for themselves in the fishing community. Joe missed the sound of their strange language, their friendliness and the fact that they did not judge him and his people.

One by one Jack and Florie's boys grew up, got jobs, found girl-friends and went off to marry and start families of their own.

Joey, the eldest, married Dorothy from Lansdowne and they stayed with her mother Annie in a cottage on Chinaman Lee Pan's property in Lansdowne Road close to grandfather Joe's home.

John married Bertha, also from the area. They stayed with her family in a cottage on Racecourse Road, in the years before it became a freeway. In the 1950s, when the City Council officials started going around asking if people wanted to put their names down for houses in Bridgetown in Athlone, they filled in the forms to move there. All their friends were moving there too.

The McBain great-grandchildren were born one after the other, and they were all loved and cherished. But amid the bright spots, there were so many disappointments, so much sadness and fear, especially after the National Party swept into power in 1948. They soon began to implement their segregationist apartheid policies. Joe McBain followed these stories in the newspapers and could not foresee a happy outcome for his family.

In July 1950 the gavel fell: the Group Areas Act was promulgated in parliament. The period of forced removals had arrived and it would last into the early 1980s.

William, the third brother, married Roma from Newlands. They joined the New Apostolic Church as part of their new identity, on the way to being reclassified white in the mid-1950s. If they could become white they could evade the forced removals and stay in Newlands.

Rose married Gerry from Dale Street and in time gave birth to the much-cherished James and Linda. And Joe cried in his heart, along with Sophie, Florie and the girls, when they announced the sale of their house in Chelsea Village, Wynberg. They had also decided to be reclassified white and would be moving to Johannesburg.

Then Cousin Dolly, who had never married, announced that she was leaving for England. They all wanted better lives, they said, instead of being stuck on the 'wrong' side of the apartheid laws.

Joe couldn't help thinking, 'What is wrong with this life? Are we that bad, that skin colour is more important than family? Yes, their father didn't do right by them, but to take such a drastic step to find distance?'

Doreen, the eldest of the daughters, never married. Stella, the second youngest, had been planning to become a teacher when she suddenly decided to quit school after Standard 9. She ended up working in Bawa's Shop in Chichester Road, Claremont. She had a boyfriend, Wilfred Coetzee, who finished matric at Livingstone High School in Claremont and went to UCT to study for

Dor and Mavie snapped outside the Movie Snaps, Darling Street, City Centre, 1950s.

a science degree. He obtained a teaching diploma as well and became a high school teacher.

Jack and Joey both admired his profession and facetiously called him Meneer Wilfie, overlooking his brusqueness and his moodiness.

Mavie, the baby of the family, made them all proud when she went to study nursing at Somerset Hospital. Jack did not pay for her college fees, but family friends, Mr and Mrs Frances, insisted that they would do the honours.

In the mid-1950s Mavie McBain and Ivan Davids, a high school classmate, became a couple. Nursing was a noble profession, the elders agreed, but what's with the boyfriend? Joey, her oldest brother, said outright there was something strange about that *ou*.

'The man just talks about himself all the time. "I, I, I ... I did

Right: *Ivan and Mavie on Table Mountain, 1950s.*

Opposite L-R: *Stella, Mavie, Grandma Florie and her school friend Mrs Grover from USA; Mrs Williams from Dale Street; Ivan and Dor.*

this and I did that." I'm keeping my eye on him,' he griped. He never made a secret of his dislike of his youngest sister's choice. The old ladies, Sophie and Florie, were charmed though. Ivan sat and talked to them, made tea for them and served it with the pomp and ceremony that should accompany *every* cup of tea, he insisted. He dressed well, spoke well, and his shoes shone from polishing. He was well-mannered and even sang hymns with them, although he was not a churchgoer.

To Mavie, he complained endlessly about his family. Especially how his mother never loved him and one of his younger brothers. He said it was his misfortune that he was like a cat, gravitating towards those who felt no affinity with him. Mavie understood this bitterness in Ivan. After all, she'd been rejected by her father.

Incidentally, Florie and Jack knew his mother, Christina (formerly Adams). She'd grown up in Newlands. She started in the Salvation Army and in time transitioned to the Anglican Church. Christina had never liked Florie, because she simply could not tolerate *'halwe naartjies'* (half breeds) like her. The actual word was *nasies* – nations – interesting turns of phrase were created in the Cape community.

Right: *Ivan and Mavie snapped by a neighbour who spotted them in Mouille Point before Mavie returned to the nurses' residence at Somerset Hospital, 1950s.*

Opposite: *My baptism certificate from the newly opened Our Lady Help of Christians Church in Lansdowne, 1961.*

Christina was of Javanese slave descent, she often said. Yet only the odd Afrikaans word passed her lips. She only spoke the King's – later the Queen's – English and sounded very lah-di-dah. She played her black upright piano when she wasn't crocheting the finest of garments and tableware. She had ten children and she divorced her husband Charles, also of South-East Asian descent, in the 1950s. They lived in a semi-detached house The Oval in 30 Chichester Road, Claremont, next to Bawa's Shop.

The irony was that at least five of Christina's grandchildren produced *'halwe-naartjies'*, on three continents, and some have transitioned to other religions.

After Christina's divorce from Charles, Ivan never had contact with his father again, and Mavie never met him. According to gossip, Charles was a peacock of a man who painted landscapes in oils and played tennis. When he won, he would parade up and down Chichester Road in his all-white tennis gear. When he lost, his family bore the brunt of his bad sportsmanship.

Joe watched and waited for the changes that would inevitably come to his family.

Then Sophie had a stroke, her bad temper finally catching up with her. After she died in 1958, the silence was so deafening that it killed Joe a mere two months later. The doctor said he'd died of old age though – Joe was in his eighties.

Jack inherited his father's property. Now what? What would happen, where would Florie and the girls – Doreen, Stella and Mavie – go?

Her oldest son Joey said sell 'the *bladdie* house', but John and William vetoed that idea, sensing their mother's anxiety. And so the house was not sold and everybody stayed.

Mavie married Ivan in July 1960 at the Catholic Chapel on Lansdowne Road. They wanted to rent a place of their own in Kromboom, but the ever-anxious Florie, fearing for her daughter and for herself, asked them to stay. She'd heard the rumours about Ivan's father, just like everybody else, and she worried that his son would be like his father.

I was born in June 1961 at home in Heatherley Road, delivered by Nurse Hansen. Grandpa Jack, Grandma Florie, Aunties Stella

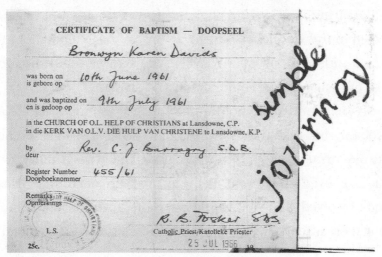

and Dor (my appointed godmother), Uncle Joey and even the always-cross Meneer Wilfie all doted on Bronnie. They all had a new toy to play with and I had lots of visitors.

'What the hell!' Ivan was said to have exclaimed just after my birth. 'She has a *bladdie* crown of thorns on her head. Look how it stands up. And look at the button nose. Have you ever seen anything like it?'

It was to be my first inkling about how important appearance and looks were to the community I had been born into. Coloureds were weird that way: they'd roll an imaginary dice and take bets on what a pregnancy would deliver. Would it come out dark to the fair, or fair and blue-eyed to the dark? Everybody maliciously waited for dark children to be visited on fair relatives, especially those who had opted to be reclassified white.

And then the offspring all go through a lifetime of the vicious game of *trek die siel uit?* which entailed drawing out the child's 'spirit' to ascertain temperament. They would tease and mock and provoke, a disruptive and unnecessary thing to do. After which the poor kid would be boxed in by the often-repeated line of 'you take after so and so'.

Labelling is very limiting, and it was unpleasant to be subjected to *trek die siel uit?* by grownups in the extended family. It was a nuisance, especially when you had better things to do, like playing outside, colouring-in and drawing.

My own family did not taunt and tease as much as outsiders, probably because they were too busy with all kinds of chores. My older cousins popped out fair, dark, in-between, dark, blonde and blue-eyed (times two), medium, medium, medium, fair, blond and blue-eyed, and so it would alternate until there was me and four more after me who were all similarly varied. The blond and blue-eyed cousins were unpretentious coloureds who lived in Bridgetown.

My looks attracted much comment, some quite nasty, mostly from females in great-grandma Sophie's family. They thought I may have Down syndrome or cerebral palsy. I was always sickly. On top of which I didn't resemble anyone in either my mother or my father's families.

Seeing that they had so much to say, they might have urged Mavie to ask Dr Cliffie Louw to check me out for autism. It might have satisfied their need to label me. We certainly travelled the distance to Athlone often enough for a snotty nose, tonsillitis and all other childhood diseases. I stoically endured the stick stuck on the tongue and the 'Say ahh' or the occasional injection of antibiotics. My consolation was to admire the front garden at the surgery with its fountain and fishpond. When Dr Louw emigrated to Canada, we went to Drs Sakinofsky and Osrin's surgery where Dor worked. And still no further tests for whatever was 'wrong' with me.

Make no mistake, appearances always came first in the community I grew up in. People contradicted themselves when they quoted the English proverb, 'Do not judge a book by its cover'. I suppose this applied only to some and not others.

Ivan's suspicions about my oddity were confirmed when I grew into toddlerhood and started talking. I acquired an imaginary friend named Dali. I received dark looks of censure and he'd snap at me to stop.

I had only two years with Grandma Florie before her life of broken-heartedness consumed her. She died at Groote Schuur Hospital while in a diabetic coma. I wanted her back. I devised all kinds of plans to get her back out of that place in the sky I'd been told she'd gone to. These included the use of the very tall extension ladder which had to be placed on Grandpa Jack's crock VW Kombi.

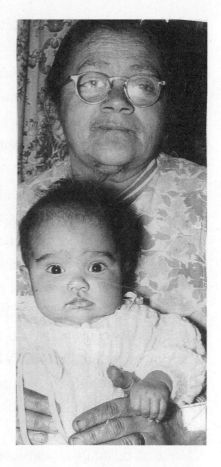

The day she died in April 1963, her departing spirit endured its final humiliation at the hands of Grandpa Jack and Miss Lizzie. The mistress had never met Grandma Florie, who had decided never to play into their hands by acting out the role of the confrontational scorned wife. Mavie and Stella heard from a reliable source that on the day Grandpa Jack told Miss Lizzie that his wife had died, the two of them laughed until the tears rolled down their faces, and streaks ran down Miss Lizzie's carefully powdered and rouged face.

About six months after Grandma Florie's death Ivan, who was a badge designer at Mr Barlow's embroidery factory in Steenberg, quit his job. He signed up for a six-month season working on the Dutch whaling vessel, the *Willem Barends*. At the age of 32, he worked as a deckhand, aiding in the hunting and killing of whales in the South Atlantic. The meat was destined for the European and Asian markets.

Ivan must have hated being at sea because he never went back when the season ended but resumed his job at Barlow's. His stories were filled with the horrors of the Roaring Forties (the strong westerly winds of the Southern Hemisphere between latitudes of 40 and 50 degrees), fear of imminent death, of vomit overboard, horrible shipmates who had murderous intent to push him overboard, their foul language, and the gore and blood everywhere on deck, which was his responsibility to clean up.

Grandpa Jack was still living in two places: at Miss Lizzie's all day, sleeping at Heatherley Road at night. After 33 years of defiant togetherness, he and Miss Lizzie only married in the mid-1960s, about three years after Grandma Florie's death, at St Paul's. Finally, he moved to her rented house in Belgravia Estate in Athlone.

Miss Lizzie's family had lived in Black River, but it was declared a white area and they'd been forced to leave their home in the 1950s and move to the Cape Flats.

Left: *Uncle Kenny, not long before he died, 1996.*

Opposite: *Grandma Florie and me with my crown of thorns, 1961.*

Dor, Stella and Mavie only met Miss Lizzie, who had been a dark shadow in their lives for so long, the day Kenny married Olive from Simonstown. The wedding tea was held at the house in Heatherley Road. Dor and Stella were polite, but Mavie – who'd been cruelly rejected by her father to pacify his mistress – refused to be diplomatic and ignored her.

By 1966, only five people lived in great-grandpa Joe's house: my mother Mavie, her husband Ivan, and me, and Mavie's two older sisters Dor and Stella. But there was always an assortment of visitors in for short stays. The four grownups contributed to a pool which covered upkeep of the property, rates, electricity, water and food.

Each one saved the rest of their meagre wages and used it to buy what was perceived as uplifting things. They surely needed it as a way to help them deal with apartheid. By now, its laws had become the bane of their existence.

Above: *Ivan, Mavie and me at my first birthday party, 1962.*

Opposite: *Dor and me in the lounge, 1963.*

Above: *Mavie and me in mourning for Grandma Florie, standing in the straggly vegetable patch, 1963.*

Opposite top L-R: *My first birthday party, friend Jean Engelbrecht, Grandma Florie, Mavie and me, Dor, friend Mrs Maggie Smith, Stella.* Standing: *Ivan, cousins Flo-Anne and Gregory, and Mr Peter Smith, 1962.*

Opposite bottom: *At cousin Esme's home, where Cavendish Square is today, for her daughter Denise's first birthday party, 1963.*

Above L-R: *Me at my second birthday party; having breakfast on the road to Goedverwacht; and all dressed up for the double wedding in Goedverwacht.*

Opposite: *Me on the purloined, old rusty bicycle in the yard. The old part of the garage can be seen in the background, 1964.*

Top: *View of the Heatherley house from Dale Street, 1976.*

Bottom: *Mavie's room at 62 Ajax Way, Woodlands, 1993.*

Home, sugary home

THERE WAS NOTHING ordinary about the house and garden great-grandpa Joe had conjured into being and everybody else had added to over time. It wasn't a grand house – it was an expressionist work of art.

The textures of my childhood home fed the imagination: the wood-framed sash windows, painted wooden shutters on the outside, the rows of African violets and a few cacti in pots with their *perlemoen* shells as saucers on the windowsills. These served as protection in *lieu* of burglar bars. Who had burglar bars and security gates then? Some people didn't even lock their doors.

There was nothing quite like sitting at the open sash window at the small four-seater table in the kitchen, eating lunch or doing homework or listening to Springbok radio with Mavie, and being able to look out over the garden.

I liked our doors: the always-open blue-grey stable door, the painted wooden doors to the rooms with their round brass knobs, the patterns on the sand-blasted glass panes on either side of the seldom-used-front door, and the pane in the door itself which let afternoon light into the passage.

My favourite door was the one between the kitchen and the lounge. The bottom was wooden, while the top had different coloured glass panes in a frame. All mismatched, of course. I'm sure there was solid oak under the layers of paint. The floors were made of suspended tongue-and-groove teak planks.

We seldom used the lounge and dining room, except for parties and sometimes weddings. The old house was a one-stop space for weddings because photos could be taken in the lush garden with all its odd twists of beauty.

On the evenings before functions, I could explore the layers of time when the two sideboards and cupboards were unlocked to reveal what nestled within. Every bowl, tea set, plate, glass, knife, fork, ladle, spoon, cake fork and pudding *bakkie* had history attached of who it belonged to, either great-grandmothers Sophie and Minnie or Grandma Florie. Great-grandpa Joe's Bible stood on the 'newer', circa 1940s, sideboard.

There were also many gifts from old friends – brass candlesticks, souvenirs from far-away places. And beautiful cranberry glass lamps, with fresh wick and oil in them, stood like sentries on one sideboard, in case of electricity failure in winter.

The drawers held linen tablecloths and napkins and an assortment of lace cloths. There were yellowing Belgian lace cloths made by Grandma Florie, and crocheted cotton doilies, tablecloths and tea-tray cloths made by Ivan's mom Christina, whom I called Granny Davids.

My favourite things were the old Christmas decorations. There were colourful wooden ornaments, clay angels, Christmas lights from the 1950s and shiny, new baubles. That part of the sideboard smelled of Christmas. The old artificial Christmas tree was the kind with tiny cups at the end in which to stick-thin candles. The candles were for decoration rather than to light.

What should have been the front entrance of the old, ramshackle house was never used. There must have been a gate at one stage, but it disappeared into a cheerful towering hedge of black-eyed Susan, English ivy, bougainvillea and morning glory that tangled into each other's foliage in the shared space.

On the veranda, the windows were overgrown by the Hoya creeper with its pink bouquets of tiny waxy flowers. All kinds of treasures were kept on the veranda: hurricane lamps, wicker baskets, an assortment of oak furniture that had been Great-grandpa José Antonio's, cupboards with books, battered trunks with ornaments, old chairs, and a concrete shelf with pot plants.

In those cupboards on the veranda, I found evidence of Grandpa Jack's household rule that only English should be spoken. And only encyclopaedias, good novels, newspapers, *Women's Own* and *National Geographic* were allowed as reading matter. There was an outright ban on the reading of comics. I was also discouraged from reading comics, but before I could read, Dor would relate to me the adventures of a bird named Robin in a comic strip in the British magazine *Women's Own*.

In spite of Grandpa Jack's ban, Afrikaans was freely used for colour, emphasis and exclamation. Some things were best said in Afrikaans. Like if you needed to tell someone off or *skel* them, you'd throw in an Afrikaans swear word or two. It had the effect of the hounds of hell being unleashed.

The cupboards were also filled with an assortment of Bibles, catechism books and hymnals. Games – such as rings, cards, dominoes and darts that the uncles and their friends used to play in the kitchen, or the yard – were still there, neat in their boxes. It seems the house was full when the boys were still single, in spite of Grandpa Jack's no alcohol rule, which everybody respected.

The contents of the cupboards, though decades old, were still intact and had not suffered any water damage. The veranda remained dry and dusty through every winter.

In winter, the zinc roof of the house leaked no matter how many times the gutters and the chimney were cleaned and in spite of all holes being sealed before the rains came. The leaks were always on the eastern part of the house where it had been extended and were probably back-flow from the gutters.

But not even basins all over the floor to catch the dripping water could deter visitors. Always the warmth from the wood-stove made up for the inconvenience of stepping around the basins. Everybody came in through the kitchen door and plonked themselves down at one of the two tables. The chairs were an assortment of oak, cane and the latest Formica and metal chairs, and they were all adorned with comfy cushions. Some nights, the aunties' friends from the neighbourhood came by to do crafts. They embroidered, crocheted, knitted or made raffia bags. Visitors would sometimes draw up a chair to sit beside the stove where cooking and baking fragrances lingered.

Every castle has its crown jewel, something that pulls the whole building together and gives it a reason for existing. Our jewel at Great-grandpa Joe's castle was an eight-plate, pale-blue wood and coal Jewel stove with a warmer shelf at the top and a water boiler on the side.

The Jewel stood on a plinth, enclosed on three sides by walls. The wall in the corner formed a section where wood was stacked in a Bashew's cooldrink box. Brooms, mops, long feather dusters, spades, a rake, a pitchfork and other gardening tools stood behind it. There was also a little shelf for wood under the extended boiler section of the stove.

Logs were delivered every week by the wood merchant Mr Dodgen, and these were split smaller by either Ivan or Uncle Joey. I think they just liked splitting logs to vent their frustrations.

The fire was started at five o'clock every morning and fed throughout the day and left to die down late. The ash was cleared out of the burner once it had cooled, either the same night or the next morning.

With a collective gravitational pull toward 'sugar and spice and all things nice', baking was the food-related activity that everyone in the house excelled at. *Platkoeke* were often the order of the day, because the oven, which could hold four round cake pans at once, was rather temperamental and didn't always provide the desired outcome. Being a wood-burning stove, heat distribution was patchy and a jug of water had to be placed in the oven to rectify the problem.

The 22-cm sponge cakes never rose higher than three or four centimetres at the most and always split when removed from the pans. Or they imploded in the middle or they were lopsided. These imperfections were camouflaged by dollops of butter icing. Roped into kitchen duty from an early age, I became an expert butter-icing maker.

Each imperfect cake was welcomed with great enthusiasm and went down well with tea and compliments that it 'tasted really good' and 'yes, I will have another slice, thanks'. Sweet was good, salt was good, fat was good – and you only live once. So there!

Stella's speciality was coffee cake, made with an essence she guarded with her life. Her chocolate cake was light and fluffy, a genuine chocolatey melting moment. Mavie made fairy cakes, and little tarts with jam or coconut, and her Hertzoggies with a coconut meringue covering the jam. She also made crustless milk tart and tea loaves: banana, raisin, date or ginger.

For a few seasons, she did a roaring trade in rainbow-coloured, two-deck sponge cakes, selling to workers and their families at

Strandfontein beach. But that market dried up when Ivan left his job as a beach control officer and became a Divisional Council traffic cop.

Saturday was baking day. We always had lots of visitors on Saturdays, many from Claremont plus the usual neighbourhood friends. People turned up uninvited, bringing prepared but uncooked exotic snacks, like doughnuts, koeksisters and samoosas that they would fry off at our place, or a pot of warm breyani.

Ivan's speciality was watermelon or fig *konfyt,* and melon-and-ginger jam which he'd learnt to cook in his youth. Foodwise, he was the king of fry-ups. His version of *ouvrou-onder-die-kombers* consisted of leftover Sunday roast beef dipped in batter and fried.

He also made all kinds of *smoortjies* with onions, tomato, garlic polony, smoked snoek or bully beef. Unfortunately, all the frying caught up with him in the end quite suddenly at his desk at the old Regional Services Council building in Wale Street, Cape Town, in 1993. No amount of ballroom dancing and long-distance swimming from Kalk Bay to Muizenberg could offset a diet that bad.

Dor was the head gardener and chief baker. Before she became head flower arranger at Our Lady Help of Christians Catholic Church on Lansdowne Road and was too busy on Saturday afternoons, Dor was usually the one who made the bread, scones and fruit pies, all prepared with careful consideration.

She would pick loquats or guavas and stew them, make the pastry, roll it out, place in Pyrex dishes, add the stewed fruit with whole cinnamon, arrange the pastry lattice on top, brush with egg and entrust it to the oven. The pies were served with a rich golden homemade custard. Fruit from the garden was also often stewed to go with oven-baked sago or tapioca pudding.

Dor also made bread-and-butter pudding and, for special occasions, Queen's pudding. I'd crumble the white bread slices into a bowl. This she would place in a buttered stainless steel dish. She would scald milk and butter, pour it over the crumbs and let it stand for a few minutes before adding beaten egg yolk, sugar and vanilla essence. The mixture would be baked until set and then covered with jam. She'd beat the egg white until it formed peaks, add a tablespoon of sugar, mixed and spread over the jam. The dish was returned to the oven and baked until the meringue browned slightly. What a queen of a pudding!

In summer she made fruit salad with fruits from the garden plus pawpaw and bananas, which she bought. 'The pawpaw is what makes the salad taste so great,' she always said.

Stella made pineapple pudding, which consisted of a tin of Ideal milk, pineapple jelly and a tin of pineapple pieces, blitzed together and left to set in the fridge.

No, we did not have cake and pudding every day. These luxuries were for weekends. For the rest of the week, we had home-made left-over cake and coconut biscuits and store-bought Marie Biscuits and Ouma rusks. They were usually dipped in sweet, milky tea or coffee. The top of the movable, almost two-metre-long kitchen dresser was packed with great numbers of colourful old biscuit tins for the storage of cake and biscuits.

Real, cooked food was incidental in the grand scheme of things. 'If we could eat pudding first, we would,' Uncle Joey often quipped with his own brand of irreverence. And sometimes one or the other of them would indeed take a dip into the pudding *bakkie* first.

Mavie kept her cooking plain but flavourful with mixed herbs or thyme, bay leaves, salt and white pepper, nutmeg, cloves or cinnamon, depending on the dish. Everything had a smoky flavour

LEMON MERINGUE.

Take 16 Marie biscuits. Roll to fine crumbs and mix with ¼ lb. melter butter. Pat it smoothly into a pyrex flan dish.

Drain ℓ tin sweetened condensed ℓk into basin. Add the yolks from two eggs and beat well into conden milk. Add ½ cup lemon ce plus a little of the grated lemon rind and beat well again. Pour mixture over the Marie biscuit base. Whip the egg whites until they stand in peaks. Fold in gently 3 tablespoons sugar and smooth this over the condensed milk mixture. Bake in slow oven 275° for 2 — 2½ hours until meringue topping is crisp and golden brown.

Mrs. B. Grindley,
Simonstown.

LEMON MERINGUE PIE.

1 tin sweetened condensed milk.	2 eggs separated.
½ cup lemon juice.	2 tablespoons granulated sugar.
Grated rind of 1 lemon.	Baked pie shell (8 inches).

Mix together sweetened condensed milk, lemon juice and grated lemon rind and the egg yolks. Pour into baked pie shell. Cover with meringue made by beating egg whites until stiff and adding sugar.

Bake in a mod. oven (350°) for 10 minutes or until meringue is brown. Chill before serving.

Mrs. N. Williams.
Clarem
enilworth

Sponge Cake

gs.	1 small cup milk.
ps flour.	1½ small cups sugar.
zs. butter.	1 teaspoon vanilla.
level teaspoons B.P.	

Beat eggs and sugar well together. Add sifted flour. Add boiling butter and milk, and lastly, B.P. and vanilla. Cook in 375° oven for about 15 minutes, in two 9" well-greased cake pans.

ICING.

2 ozs. butter.	1½ cups icing sugar.
Juice of half orange.	

Soften butter, add icing sugar, then orange juice and colouring if desired.

Miss B. M. Nowlan,
Heathfield.

SPONGE LAYER CAKE.

ar.	3 teaspoons Royal B.P.
spoons butter or margarine.	1¾ cups flour.
cold water ×¼ cup	Pinch salt.
3 eggs.	Vanilla essence.

Cream butter and sugar, then add the three beaten egg-yolks and beat very well. Add the cold water and beat again. Sift flour, salt and B.P. and add. Lastly fold in the three stiffly beaten egg whites and 1 teaspoon vanilla essence. Bake in 2 greased sandwich cake tins ° for 20 minutes. Sandwich together with mock cream.

Above and opposite: *Mavie's most used recipes from the* Salesians Boys' School Recipe Book, *1960s.*

SAVOURY RICE.
(Supper Dish).

4 rashers of bacon.
1 tin Mac's button mushrooms.
2 sheep's kidneyys.
1 large onion.

2 tablespoons butter.
1 cup rice.
1 lb. peas.

Dice the bacon, kidneys and onion. Fry in butter until tender. Drain liquid off mushrooms — add to mixture until well heated. Cook the rice, and also the peas.

Serve the savoury mixture on a meat dish, surrounded by a ring of peas, and then a ring of rice. The extra rice can be served in an extra bowl.

This mixture cannot spoil in keeping warm for an hour or two, even improves the flavour.

Mrs. T. Shenfield,
Simonstown.

SPANISH RICE.

Wash and thoroughly dry rice and fry to a light golden brown colour, with onions, garlic and chillies (Quantity according to taste) Now add a tin of tomato soup and cook the rice in the ordinary way. When ready a little strong cheese may be sprinkled over. Garnish with rings of fresh green peppers.

Mrs. M. Milidachi.
Kenilworth

from the woodstove and this gave the food a unique taste. That stove provided slow cooking at its best, although Mavie was not a fan of its erratic ways. She had great battles with it: slamming lids and letting off a litany of swear words quite often. The cleaning of all the movable parts was a sooty business and was cause for more f and b words.

The sisters were in their 20s and early 30s and they too wanted to be able to cook fast on an electric stove. But the electric cabling in the house was old and because of the uncertainty of the Group Areas removals, which were now in full swing, they did not want to go through the expense of re-cabling to a new electricity box.

Instead, Stella used the gas stove that she had for camping. Her favourite camping spot was Duikersklip before the Hangberg flats were built to the top of the dip, just before the rise of

Hout Bay Sentinel. She, Meneer Wilfie and her friends would climb over to the rocky bay on the other side, which was very popular for *kreef*-diving. We went along for day trips but never stayed over.

Stella would also use the gas stove on countrywide road trips with her friends. She cooked only at weekends, after work on a Saturday. When she came back from her travels, she would cook dishes she had learned about. A peri-peri prawn dish with cashews and rice with saffron, after she'd been to Mozambique and Yorkshire pudding to go with the Sunday roast after she'd been to England.

Her travels also led to us receiving lots of holidaymakers: Indian Hindu and Tamil friends from Durban, Pietermaritzburg and Pinetown, and once some Portuguese people from Lourenco Marques who came to Cape Town to see if they wanted to stay here. They chose Rio de Janeiro instead after Mozambique gained independence in 1975 from Portugal, the colonial power that had governed the territory for five centuries. They got out before the civil war erupted.

Mavie cooked all the traditional meals that everyone was cooking at the time. For breakfast, Jungle Oats or mielie meal porridge – and Weetbix for those can't-be-bothered days. For supper, she cooked all the bredies (green beans, tomato, cabbage), *frikkadels*, cabbage-wrapped *frikkadels,* liver in tomato sauce, sugar beans stew, Irish stew, mince-and-pea curry with white rice, spaghetti bolognaise and *bobotie.* Lunch was usually leftovers or a sandwich with tea.

For special occasions on weeknights, there was pot roast brisket (cheaper than lamb chops in the 60s and 70s), pot roast beef or pot roast chicken. Chicken was a luxury because it cost more

Top: *Climbing Table Mountain – Stella, Dor, Ivan and Mavie, 1950s.*

Bottom: *One of the Lansdowne Anglican Churches picnics to Churchhaven.*
L-R: *Dor, Mr Smith, Mrs Smith, Meneer Wilfie, me, Stella,*
Mavie and neighbour, Mrs Ivy, 1964.

Top: *At the beach, back row: Stella, Mavie, Uncle Julian.* Front L-R: *Mrs Ivy, cousins Marlene and Lorna, me and Ivan, 1962.*

Bottom: *Mavie on the rocks at Mouille Point, 1950s.*

than red meat. All were served with squash, cauliflower with white sauce, roast potatoes and yellow rice. Rustic soups enriched with soup bones full of marrow, vegetables and barley were winter highlights, followed by pumpkin fritters with sugar and cinnamon.

Sometimes there was corned beef or homemade steak 'n kidney pie with boiled potatoes or mash, salad made with tomato, onion and lettuce and squash with mustard as the accompanying condiment. Macaroni cheese or savoury rice with a tomato-onion-lettuce salad was always paired with breakfast sausage or minute steaks. Lamb chops or fish fillets or *kuite* (fish roe or fish eggs that look like sausages) came with potato chips and a tomato and onion smoor.

I didn't eat the *kuite* or rollmops. I also drew the line at giblets stew, homemade brawn, tripe and trotter curry. But I did eat *kaiings* though, made from the excess fat cut from the meat, chopped into tiny bits and cooked in a pot until crispy. So lekker. 'Lekker', by the way, was without a doubt the most-used Afrikaans word in our family.

My favourite was when Mavie made bredies. Just after the meat and onions had browned (or burnt and she had done a quick rescue mission), before the veg was added, she would call me in from playing outside for *brood-in-die-pot* and tea. A slice of bread was put into the pot to cook a few minutes and it absorbed the browned fat and onion juices. It was very lekker.

All the lard was stored in containers in the fridge and used for cooking. Even the excess fat from Sunday roast was saved and used again for the bredies. Uncle Joey would visit most days and head straight for the bread bin for a slice or two of bread, spread with fat and topped off with whatever leftover meats or spreads and jams were around. (He wasn't supposed to eat those. Doctor's orders. He had diabetes.)

Then there was the Christian ritual of Good Friday pickled fish from a recipe that was invented and shared by Cape Malay slaves[4]. Hot cross buns were always bought – I don't think my family had a recipe for them. We ate the same menu for Easter Sunday as we did for Christmas, except without the Christmas *doekpoeding*. We had one of the usual winter puddings, usually with custard.

Easter weekend was more about church than food, although I got the impression that chocolate may just have sneaked into first place ahead of piousness for some. The Easter holy week began on Palm Sunday with the handing out of palm crosses that

---

4   In the Catholic, Eastern Orthodox, Anglican and Methodist Christian denomi-
    nations, the Friday Fast is the practice of abstaining from eating warm-blooded
    animal meat on Fridays throughout the year, on the Fridays of Lent and on Ash
    Wednesday, when meat is replaced with cold-blooded fish. The practice has been
    upheld since the first century AD when early Christians ate fish to commemo-
    rate the crucifixion of Jesus which took place on a Friday. Fast forward to the
    seventeenth century Cape of Good Hope where the Dutch East India Company
    (VOC) started a colony to supply fresh produce to ships sailing to the East.
    Slaves were brought from the East and from the rest of Africa to work on the
    farms. Among these slaves were Malay fishermen who reportedly created the
    ingelegde vis (pickled fish) recipe to preserve their autumn catch. The original
    recipe is still in use today, but with many variations handed down from genera-
    tion to generation. As the mixed-heritage slave population grew into emancipa-
    tion in 1838, with many who accepted Christianity as their religion, pickled fish
    became the dish of choice on Good Friday. The recipe consists of fish squares
    fried separately and set aside. Older recipes up to the 1940s suggest geelbek (Cape
    Salmon), while modern recipes use any white fish. A sauce of onion rings, turme-
    ric, curry powder, chillies (optional), salt, pepper, bay leaves, sugar, peppercorns,
    vinegar and water is boiled up and then reduced by half. The fish squares are
    added in layers to this mixture. The dish is made at least two days before Good
    Friday and is served cold with fresh bread or hot cross buns and butter.
    Godoy, M. 06 April 2012. *Lust, Lies and Empire: The Fishy Tale Behind Eating Fish on Friday*.
    NPR News. 2012/04/05/150061991/lust-lies-and-empire-the-fishy-tale-behind-eating-fish-
    on-Friday. Last accessed 03/03/2020.

symbolised Jesus' entry into Jerusalem, riding on the back of a donkey over a street that had been covered with cloaks and beside which people stood waving palm fronds.

The weekend began on Thursday with the blessing of the anointing oils, holy water, wine, wafers, paschal candles and incense, all of which were to be used throughout the archdiocese for the rest of the year. Thursday evening there'd be a special service during which the priest washed the feet of fellow clergy, deacons and lay ministers. In recent years, some churches have introduced a paschal meal after the service, as an attempt to re-imagine what Jesus did the night before he was crucified.

Good Friday was sombre with the re-enactment of the Fourteen Stations of the Cross held in the field behind the church. I found this frightening and sad. It was as if one was right there in Jerusalem all those thousands of years ago, especially if the weather was overcast and gloomy.

The re-enactment required the congregation follow, according to European processional traditions, a narrator reading passages from the Gospels. This was a shorter service than the three-hour focus on gospel readings, solemnity and prayer for adults in the afternoon. Between these two church services, there was much munching on pickled fish and buns in homes across the city.

The midnight mass, called a wake mass, was held on the eve of Easter Sunday. For me, it was the most beautiful event on the church calendar. It was dramatic from the moment one entered the darkened church where the only light came from candles flickering on the altar.

The priests and altar servers would enter in silent procession without the characteristic pipe-organ music and hymn. An altar server walked ahead carrying the incense burner. There would be opening prayers after which we filed out to hear another prayer while standing around an enormous fire. Then the paschal candle, studded with religious symbols, would be lit.

Back in the church, we would all receive light from this paschal candle to light our little white candles in cardboard holders. The paschal candle would stay lit until Pentecost. There'd be a benediction with incense, and prayers would be sung as was the tradition of the Solemn or High Mass. Only *then* would the lights be switched on for the continuation of the mass with hymns sung to the accompaniment of the pipe organ.

These were all symbolic of Jesus Christ's resurrection from the grave – rising out of darkness on the third day. The tradition goes back centuries to the days when Christians could not read the Gospels for themselves and the stories were told through images, symbolism and re-enactment. Going to this mass felt like touching the ancient past.

All Holy days, events and foods went according to the seasons, except at Christmas, when we ate a traditional British meal, as was the custom at the Cape since colonial times. Girls were taught all these dishes by their mothers and in Domestic Science classes at high school, out of a 1948 textbook called *Housecraft for Primary Schools* by R Fouche and WM Currey. Often new recipes were swopped or cut out of newspapers and British magazines.

The Christmas meal was oven-roasted leg of lamb with potatoes flavoured with a sectioned onion. The meat (always carved by Dor) was served with cauliflower and white sauce, gem squash and yellow rice, gravy and Dor's mint leave salad, with chopped onion, salt, pepper and a dash of vinegar.

The flagship of the meal was always the *doekpoeding* made days before. Making it was a long process that began with freshening up the calico cloth in which the pudding was boiled. The batter consisted of breadcrumbs, fruit mix and nuts (bought at Wellington's Fruit Growers in Darling Street in the city centre), flour, eggs, yellow sugar, a little milk, measures of mixed spice, all-spice and cinnamon. The calico would be spread over a colander and the mixture spooned in, before being tied with string and lowered into a big pot of boiling water at the bottom of which was a plate to hold the pudding's shape and to prevent it from sticking to the pot. There it would steam for five hours.

The Christmas pudding was served with custard and it would last for days. Mavie did not add coins or brandy, as was the tradition. She would not be caught dead buying brandy, and she feared that coins would lead to choking.

On Christmas day, the usual visitors would drop by after the morning service before they went off to their own family lunch. They'd be served Bashew's, the cooldrinks delivered to the door in wooden crates on Friday nights, or tea, and tarts or fruit cake.

On Christmas Eve we always went to the magical midnight mass at Our Lady Help of Christians. Carols were sung before the High Mass and were followed by a benediction. When I was still a child, Mavie would take me to the morning service.

A big part of the rituals of Christmas and Easter was to go to Klip Cemetery in Grassy Park to put flowers on the McBain family grave, after which we walked over to the grave of Great-grandpa José Antonio and Great-grandma Minnie, near the World War II soldiers' graves. Dor's flower arrangements were of such a high standard they could have easily been used as centrepieces at a bride's table or on a cathedral side altar. Her work was showcased far and wide, including at the flower festival at St Mary's Cathedral. In the 1980s she received, during Pope John Paul II's reign, two papal medals for her work in the church.

We also made a point of going to greet Uncle Joey and his family.

After 1970 – when Ivan learnt to drive and acquired a car and I was nine – we would attend Christmas tea in Claremont with his family. His brothers, who all played musical instruments, usually had an impromptu jam session, belting out jazz standards. Aunty Doreen and Granny Davids served apple tart and cream, Granny's fruit cake (which did have brandy in it) and her homemade ginger beer, and an assortment of savouries.

The big, all-out party was on January 1, the first day of the new year and also Mavie's birthday. That party lasted all day and evening and visitors just pitched, no invites.

The day before, a feast would be prepared. Tarts and sponge cakes were baked. Vegetables were grated and bagged to make bowls of salad the next morning. Corned meats were cooked. A day or two earlier smoked turkeys and cold meats were collected from Ken Higgins, the butcher. Savouries were made just before the guests arrived.

It was always a big surprise to see who would turn up. Some guests only saw each other on that day every year, but they fell into conversation with ease, picking up where they'd left off the previous year.

In spite of the forced removals happening all over Cape Town, community spirit prevailed in the older, more established areas. As apartheid's grip tightened, this community spirit seemed to obtain greater significance, perhaps a matter of the star burning brightest before it faded.

Mavie did her duty to help the sick and elderly in her family and those she knew in the community. This included changing

Mavie outside the nurses' residence at Somerset Hospital, Green Point, 1950s.

wound dressings, bathing an elderly cancer-ridden woman, and giving daily injections to a teacher friend who had tuberculosis in the fallopian tubes. Sometimes, Mavie's duties extended to laying out of the dead, just after the doctor and priest had been there, and before the undertakers turned up.

It was a way to use the nursing skills she learnt at Somerset Hospital. She often said she would have preferred to still be a nurse, but once she took a breather from nursing (after a crippling bout of anxiety during her final oral exams) there was always something that kept her rooted to the house in Lansdowne.

I think she missed those years living at the nurses' residence in Green Point, and she always spoke in glowing terms of her colleagues. She related many tales of that time: what it was like to work on the wards, going to see off nurses who were leaving for England, taking a Union Castle Line boat from A-berth in the harbour, and being let off Christmas Eve night shift duty to attend midnight mass at Sacred Heart in Green Point. It seems to me one always remembers those first tentative steps toward independence from family. If that time is coupled with achieve-ment, the passing of that period leads to a lifetime of nostalgia and reminiscences.

On many afternoons, neighbours would drop by unexpectedly to talk through their problems with Mavie. And there were end-less problems: teenage pregnancies, cheating husbands and fights with the in-laws.

Mostly, however, the talk revolved around the forced removals and being visited by Community Development officials. The men in white Volksies with GG number plates were the foot soldiers implementing the Group Areas Act in the suburbs. And every-body had the same worries: 'What now? Where are we going to move to?'

Some evenings at supper, if the food was too salty or had a slightly burnt flavour that Mavie's rescue missions could not hide, Ivan would say after the first forkful, 'Mrs Dennis was here,' or 'How's Alida doing?' He said he could taste in the food that they'd been.

Some of Mavie's stories were funny, like the ones about Mrs Atta's latest malapropisms. Others contained high drama narra-tives about life in the road, such as the time Mrs Mathyse chased down a *skelm w*ho tried to steal from her and gave him the hiding of his life. When the stories were personal, she wouldn't share them.

One night at supper, Dor, Stella and Ivan gasped when she told them she'd met her old high-school classmate Elsa at Queen Bess Shop. Elsa, who came originally from St Helena Island, moved to Haroldene Road, Lansdowne when she married, and then to the house she and her husband had built in Pinati Estate, still part of Lansdowne, towards the east of Lansdowne Station, which was said to be 'safe' from removals. She was pleased to have her own home and happy to be able to decorate and garden as they chose. And then she told Mavie about the grilling she'd received from a council official who came by before they moved. Elsa said the man found it inconceivable that they had plans to build and asked her if she was certain about not wanting to be added to the list. He was going from house to house, trying to ascertain the number of people who needed houses. It seemed inconceivable to him that they could afford to build and not have to rely on council housing. Mavie said that Elsa was quite adamant that she 'wouldn't live in those places they are building for the people'. It just doesn't feel right, Elsa had said.

Stella nodded. 'It is getting closer and closer.'

She said that nearly every day you'd see the white Volksies in Chichester Road. The men had come to talk to Mr Bawa and to Noor on Monday. Just the day before, Stella said, they'd been in to speak to Felicity and old Mr Henry. They told them that when they left, their houses would be demolished so that the road could be expanded. Felicity had come over to the shop in tears. Her father was sick and listening to what the men had to say made him feel worse, she'd told Stella. Felicity was convinced he wouldn't make it.

Mr Henry, Granny Davids' opposite neighbour, did indeed die sometime during the push to leave Chichester Road.

'The men were at your mother's house too, Ivan, and the old lady wouldn't open up.'

Mavie's response was her usual mantra: 'We must save every cent in order to buy and not have to go to the townships. It's better to buy.'

She saved as much as she could every week, but there was no getting away from the fact that constantly living with such stress and tension was extremely expensive. Placebos had to be purchased – we'd call it retail therapy these days – to have a positive attitude with which to keep going. To keep going kept frightening thoughts at bay, was the rationale.

During this time, around the late 1960s, Ivan got an office job with Grandpa Jack at one of the property development companies that built houses in the new suburbs, like Pinati Estate, for coloureds.

Ivan told us his colleague Wallace lived in Pinati and that it was very nice, but that he was considering moving to Australia. 'Perhaps we should think of going too.'

Dor, always quiet and hyper-sensitive, just looked at him, her eyes welling with tears. Mavie gave Ivan a withering look and Stella kept eating, swallowing her food with difficulty.

It was always upsetting to see the adults upset, and there was a lot of upset doing the rounds in those years.

When Stella's cantankerous and belligerent boyfriend Meneer Wilfie was eating with us, there was no chit-chat at the table. We would finish our food and depart for after-dinner chores.

For me, that would be drawing until I was old enough to clear the table and do the drying of dishes at the yellowing porcelain sink in the pantry. Stella did the washing up. She felt like a bossy older sister and I was the sorely put-upon little sister who would talk back out of sheer peevishness.

The kitchen wouldn't be tidy for long before there'd be someone at the door to visit. The chat would be light-hearted and amusing rather than heavy. Sometimes we just listened to serials on the radio, like the cop drama *Squad Cars* or one of the game shows like *Pick-a-box*.

Spirits had to be kept up, after all. And, of course, there'd be tea, sympathy and something sweet from a biscuit tin.

That's just the way it was.

A garden contrary

THEY MAY HAVE been the owners of their land, but my family was not rich in money. What it *was* rich in was creating magic, from the quaintness of the house's layout to the sprawling garden with all its interesting nooks and crannies.

On three of the plots, Great-grandpa Joe had planted a vegetable garden and an orchard. The latter consisted of five loquat trees, variously bearing yellow and white fruit, three fig trees (red and white varieties), four guava trees (red and white), Chinese guavas, a yellow cling peach, plum, pear, prune, five pomegranate trees, a row of quince bushes, a strawberry patch, red and white grape vines, Cape gooseberry and raspberry bushes.

The canopy of trees and the riot of boundary hedges cast a lovely shade in summer. Two oaks grown from acorns obtained from the Somerset West family gave the house its name: Two Oaks, Heatherley Road. Ivan tied a thick hessian rope swing with a wooden plank seat to one of the branches and this provided hours of entertainment for me and my friends who visited on weekends.

In all my travels, here, there and everywhere over six continents, I have never found another garden like that one. It was a true place of the imagination. Everywhere there were oddly shaped rocks or builders' offcuts. Terracotta roof tiles were used as flowerbed dividers or border and porcelain or concrete pipes became plant holders. Roses trailed up trellises, hydrangeas bloomed in summer. There were poinsettia trees, daisy bushes, stand-alone roses bushes, delicately fragrant sweet peas curling around bamboo supports, and bed upon bed of dahlias-ranunculus-snapdragons-poppies-bluebells-foxgloves-delphiniums-freesias-daffodils-irises-carnations-gladioli-petunias-pansies-hollyhocks-hyacinths.

During my childhood, the only vegetables and herbs still grown were potatoes, onions, celery, parsley, mint and tomatoes. Carrots were planted, but never saw the light of day, falling prey to marauding moles the adults plotted to annihilate with garlic, smoke bombs and flooding. Sometimes a mole catcher would be called in to do the honours and that was effective. All other attempts to get rid of the moles failed miserably.

There were snakes in the garden, harmless ones, but in all my years of having free run of the place I didn't come across any, not even when they slithered into the house through the always-open door. These occasions always led to an epic Mavie drama, but the snake was gone long before I got to see it.

The garden spilled over its hedge and chicken-wire fence boundaries into the paving-brickwork-and-concrete yard, a mish-mash. I think old Joe just created as he went along with whatever he had to hand. At the end of the garden, the chickens and Muskovies shared a run. They led an eccentric existence presided over by one of the five pomegranate trees, a pear, a plum and a peach tree. A block and tackle hung in a syringa tree that stood behind the hen house. It was used to remove crock car engines and was the reason the yard was so popular with my uncles' and cousins' friends. A vice attached to an old tree stump was part of this set-up.

A tangle of lantana, gooseberries and raspberries stood between these and a part of the yard Grandpa Jack leased to a construction company for a year. They needed the space to make
concrete moulding on two huge six-by-two-metre concrete tables,
used for the building projects in Pinati and Penlyn Estates. For
a short while, we had their watchman Wellington live on the
premises, in a shiny-new zinc shack next to the Norfolk pine tree
that stood on the 9 Dale Street plot.

When the company bought their own premises, the tables were
left behind and became an addition to our playing fields. My
chommies and I made mud cakes from white sand the builders
had left and marbleised it with black sand from the garden. We
used old cake tins to form the 'cakes' and arranged them on the
tables, all decorated with leaves from the garden.

On wilder days, my chommies and I would jump off the tables
into the branches that had been cut from the trees, much to Uncle
Joey's dismay. He would *skel* like anything, warning of broken
bones, broken necks and wheelchairs.

Joey and Mavie were cut from the same cloth. It was never a
good idea to be around when they *skelled* each other. Afterwards,
they would ignore one other for weeks on end.

Uncle Joey's *skelling* would always be about Mavie letting the
horse-and-cart scrap collectors take away the crock car parts
decorating the yard. And she would *skel* back that she was tired
of being harassed by the council people about the mess in the
yard. She was convinced that the littering would get us evicted.
She didn't want to draw unnecessary attention from the Volksie
men prowling our neighbourhood like hungry wolves.

Although they did not have the power to evict us from the
property that Grandpa Jack inherited and owned legally, the

73

Top left: *Stella on the logs with 5 Dale Street (Lansdowne) in the background.*

Top right: *Mavie coming home on her bicycle from Livingstone High School.*

Right: *Mavie in the garden, 1950s.*

Top left, L-R: *Dor, Stella and Mavie in the garden.*

Top right: *Stella in the yard with her bicycle, 1950s.*

Left, L-R: *Mavie, Stella, Mrs Ivy, Dor and friend Thelma Sheldon Gorvalla, in the garden after Grandma Florie's funeral, 1963.*

authorities would use any means to apply pressure, making life extremely uncomfortable. Many people buckled under such pressure, sold up and moved or emigrated.

Still, the garden was a merry mix, the beauty of the vegetation and trees, the remnants from construction sites and garage workshops and the animals that lived amongst it all. One mad chicken would escape the run from time to time. He chose to chase only one of the many children who had free run of our yard and garden: Grandpa Jack's *kleinniggie* Celie, who lived next door.

Uncle Joey had to run intervention until he got tired of chasing after the chicken. He ambushed the bird, wrung its neck, took the small chopper and lobbed off its head. After plucking the feathers, he singed off the rest over a fire made in an old paint drum, until it was ready for a pot-roasting on the Jewel.

The Muscovies were kept for Christmas – that was until the Ken Higgins Butchery moved into the block of shops near Queen Bess. Mavie discovered to her delight the smoked turkey that they prepared over the festive season, and that meant the end of the tradition of eating Muscovies.

Mavie used to tell everybody that while customers waited to be served, Mr Higgins, who was a popular pianist of light jazz, would 'tickle the ivories'. Most people knew of Ken Higgins because we heard his music played regularly on the radio, and some believed her. She was joking, of course. She always joked. I think it was a defence mechanism.

Way back in the 1920s, as soon as Great-grandpa Joe took ownership of the property, he'd planted a Norfolk pine. It grew to at least double-storey height, and every winter Mavie would say that one day that pine tree would blow over and crash into the Dale Street houses opposite us.

'Just where the hell are we going to get *bladdie* money to pay for the damages?' she would say, punctuating the rant with cross, puffy lips.

When the earthquake of 1969, measuring 6.3 on the Richter scale, shook the Western Cape, everybody was relieved the trees weren't uprooted, and the house did not fall down as happened in Ceres and Tulbagh.

What a drama that earthquake was! Talk was that animals in the city went nuts because they could feel the rumblings. In District Six, according to the know-it-all menfolk, the rats ran down the mountainside and congregated on Sir Lowry Road. In Lansdowne, Mavie watched her imbuia cupboards climb the walls and ran to zap me out of bed, snapping the elastic of my flannel pyjama pants in the process. She charged outside with everybody else to stand in the yard for safety.

There were endless stories after the fact of what should have been done. Some said the safest place was under a table, others said the bathroom was a good spot. I wished there was a way to stop hearing the stories. I would pull my shoulders up to my ears as though it might block out the sound. Sometimes, I bent my head far down over what I was doing so that the storytellers wouldn't see my tears. Mavie, not surprisingly, was relieved that the Norfolk pine did not crash down onto the neighbours' houses.

At the Dale Street side of the yard, Great-grandpa Joe had planted different types of bamboo as a hedge along the border: a row of cane bamboo with short leaves and, at the gate a marriage of tall bamboo with long, wild leaves at the top and a cypress hedge that refused to be tamed. These were the Norfolk pine's neighbours, and flower sellers and the best wreath makers from Waterloo Road were welcome when they came to cut off a few branches for their arrangements.

The driveway was wide and long enough for about eight to ten cars. Further up the yard was a garage. Initially, Great-grandpa Joe had built a brick garage, but in time more space was required for tools and for cars to be worked on over a pit. Thus, a wood-and-zinc extension was built around the second syringa tree.

My uncles and older cousins all fancied themselves mechanics and collected an assortment of buddies who regularly rolled up to work on their cars in the yard or the garage. The paving always had oil puddles leaked from somebody's crock or paint rays from the older cousins' spray-painting efforts.

The *pièce-de-résistance* of the fleet of cars that came and went over the years was a British-manufactured luxury 1937 Humber Snipe sedan. It was pale blue with a black top, sporting four doors and seating for eight or more. It had a bench in the middle that could be lowered for children to sit on, and pull-out trays, and a cane basket on the outside of the boot for *padkos*.

The car was always spoken of in awe. It was viewed as a prized exhibit in a national gallery whenever the garage was opened. It was the grandest car ever owned by the family.

It stood there, sans vital stainless-steel parts, until Stella and Meneer Wilfie went to London in 1974 and bought the necessary parts for Uncle Joey. Then it stood some more. When the garage was no more, it moved to Uncle Joey's yard. Only decades later did it leave the family.

I come from a long and proud heritage of crock-car ownership. I would die on the spot if ever I had to drive a big luxury car. I wouldn't know how to.

Great-grandpa Joe and Grandpa Jack were said to have owned a horse at some stage, although I don't know how true that is. But I can vouch for the existence of *Kerriehol,* the old grey Alsatian who moved in from Grandpa Jack's other home in Belgravia, where he spent the days with Lizzie. The dog lounged like royalty on the backseat of his owner's flashy but crock black-and-white wing-tipped Zephyr.

A few years later, even after he'd had a stroke, Grandpa Jack still insisted on driving that Zephyr – and he usually drove down the centre of the road. Matters got out of hand in the mid-1970s when he drove one-handed down the middle of the twisty Chapman's Peak Drive with Miss Lizzie – pouting red lips, shiny red patent leather shoes, handbag and all – snugly tucked in under his arm. This proved to be too much, and the uncles divested him of said car.

Kerriehol took up residence in our yard between the syringa tree with the block and tackle and the avocado tree that grew next to the water well and pump. He had a long chain and a nine-metre cable runner along which he rattled from time to time. The old dog had to be chained because of all the little children in the area and the yard gate always being open.

Mostly he just snoozed in his kennel or out in the sun, only to wake up when Mavie was on her way to the shops. Then he'd pull a Houdini, break free from his collar and follow her down the road, one day all the way to Shoprite. Other times she'd notice him behind her and march him back to his spot.

Past the well was a grapevine-covered pergola. At one end Stella had an aviary with an assortment of budgies and canaries, right at the entrance to the garden. At the opposite end was a gate in the wall that linked the house to the old part of the garage. The gate opened onto a wide lane that led to Heatherley Road. Here, the red-plumed parrot Polly lived in a huge hanging cage, wolf-whistling and calling 'hello, Pretty', giving everyone who ventured through that gate a big *skrik*.

My pre-school years of caring for the animals consisted of looking after the two baby tortoises that Uncle Joey brought home after their mom ended up as roadkill. I fed them green leaves. I was limited to only looking after the tortoises. I wasn't allowed to touch the birdie's cage, because when I was three I'd liberated a number of them when I opened the little gate of the cage. As I lectured the matriarch of the family's Goedverwacht friends about how the birds were fed, some of them got out. It was a mission to lure them back out of the fruit trees.

From the driveway side before the pergola began, in line with a woodshed and the tortoise enclosure, there was a big raised-wall pond. It sported goldfish and water lilies that grew so rapidly that they often had to be thinned out.

Before I was socialised into having friends of my own, older cousins all had a stint at teaching me how to play. When they weren't around, I'd sometimes ride an old tricycle that I purloined out of the garage up and down the driveway. Later on, Mavie and Ivan bought me my own tricycle, and when I outgrew that I rode a fairy cycle with training wheels. I never made the jump to big bicycles.

Eventually, I had chommies of my own, other kids who could see the benefit in befriending me. I had fruit trees and berries and a yard and a garden to play in. Because no other children were living at the house, I had this kingdom all to myself. And no, I wasn't the last of the family to be born at the house – that honour belongs to the first baby of the next generation, Uncle Joey's first grandchild. Three generations were born there from the 1920s to 1964.

The chommies arrived in my kingdom around 1966, when I was about five, probably following Celie, who was family. Celie and her mom came to stay next door with Great-grandma Sophie's brother Uncle Frank and the Henry family. Celie and her mom, who was Grandpa Jack's cousin Rona, were forced to leave their home in Steurhof as a result of the Group Areas removals. Their house had to be sold after Celie's grandmother Dienie (Great-grandma Sophie's sister) died.

Besides Cousin Celie and the neighbourhood children, other chommies joined us from time to time, but their names are now gone from memory. On weekends, visitors' children such as Sheila, Roger, Louie and many others who came by car from places like Claremont and Fairways would join us. To accommodate these children, dressed up in nice clothes for visiting and being a lot tamer than us, we stuck to skipping, hide-and-seek, and swinging in the old oak tree.

Jumping in and out of an elastic loop was a firm favourite. Two children were the supports, with a long elastic loop secured around their ankles or behind their knees, depending on how challenging it needed to be. The supporters were like goalkeepers at each end of a field. Two jumpers would jump in and out of the elastic loop. There were synchronised moves like Double Dutch and some other complicated twisting combinations, but those were far too advanced for the likes of us.

Though I played with heart and soul, I never quite got the hang of being socialised and following the rules of games, and I often questioned every decision. We played *kennetjie* where two bricks were placed parallel to each other. A stick with carved-off ends would be placed on top of the bricks. A hitter, using a cane stick cut from the hedge, would use as much force as possible to lift the carved stick in the air, and depending on where it landed, had to run cricket-like runs and not be caught out by fielders and the keeper. It was a game of skill.

The bigger boys came to play soccer in the yard, with the garage doors as one goal post and the driveway gates as the other post. They played fast and dirty, and my chommies and I were only allowed into the game because they invaded our space. I was always in defence or a goalie.

We also played our version of cricket, using a plank for a bat, a tennis ball and paint tins for wickets. And we played rounders, which was a version of baseball, only we used tomato-box planks instead of bats and a ball made of old pantihose wound tight. All our games consisted of hitting things far away, then running like crazy not to get caught out.

We loved playing school-school during the holidays. Mavie always thought we were crazy when I hauled out the blackboard Ivan had made me and a box of chalk which Meneer Wilfie had kindly donated from Vista High's school supplies.

'You're all lekker mad,' she would tell us. 'Whole term, you don't want to go to school and look what you're playing now. Don't you want to play something else?'

These were the only times she bothered about directing our games unless we were playing too close to the windows with things like sticks, bats and balls.

I always claimed the teacher spot. After all, how could children who had no inclination to read books possibly teach? I had to look out for my own intellectual well-being. The only other person I would allow to be teacher was Celie when she still lived there because I knew she read books and she came first in class at All Saints.

When we played hospital-hospital I was always the radiographer. I didn't fancy being a nurse or a doctor though I never failed to instruct the doctors and nurses on how to apply the bandages properly. I had more experience of being in hospital and going on hospital visits than all of them put together.

Sometimes we'd play housie-housie. I never wanted to be the mom, always the traveller who came from far away to visit. Playing mom was too much hard work, I reckoned.

The rules of eight-block hopscotch we never mastered, but we tried. We played marbles, though I have never understood the rules governing marbles. The slate paving or the concrete driveway always had blocks or chalk lines of outer perimeters, halfway and quarter-way lines drawn on it.

From the late 1960s, Coca-Cola and Fanta intermittently promoted their brands at primary schools, along with epic displays of dingbat moves or slick yo-yo tricks. The dingbat was an oval plastic paddle with a small rubber ball attached to it by a thin elastic. We'd watch the entertainment sipping free cooldrink and afterwards, we'd spend our pocket money savings to acquire the iconic toys for our collections.

We never played in the road, like the children further down Dale Street or Heatherley Road did. There was no need to. The yard was our refuge, a place to stay out of the way of the adults.

They perpetually inhabited a dark churning sea of problems and emotions too hard for little people to fathom.

Let hands make

ONE OF THE hardest parts of being a child was going to school – St Ignatius Primary in Claremont. School paralysed me. Playing in the yard or garden was a way to recharge my batteries after a day of stress and judgement in that institution.

At school I didn't run around, I didn't talk and I didn't make friends. I was polite when other kind children spoke to me, but I listened rather than shared anything about myself. I felt I did not belong.

It would have been better for me to go to All Saints Primary School in Lansdowne, working-class and within walking distance from our house. That way I'd have been bullied and miserable close to home at least.

But going to school in more upper-class Claremont was my inheritance from Mavie and her siblings. First St Ignatius and then on to Livingstone High School. This formulation sounded a lot like one of the death notice in the newspapers' hatch, match and dispatch columns which were Mavie's favourite daily read in both the *Cape Times* and the *Cape Argus*: 'And the funeral service for the deceased will be held at St Ignatius Primary School and thence to Livingstone High School for burial.'

Mavie would sit and read the classifieds in the evening while the rest of us were doing crafts. Ever-irreverent Mavie always prided herself on taking a year to knit Ivan's jerseys. Decades later, she embraced knitting more enthusiastically when she needed to earn extra money, knitting baby wear that sold pretty well. 'Holly ha!' she would exclaim, suddenly. 'Look who passed away.' This would be followed by 'Do you remember' or 'You know her, man! They lived in Denver Road. Ten girls and one boy.'

In spite of all my fears and hang-ups, which should have been treated by a child psychiatrist had there been any around back then, I did well at school. I was always in the top ten in class, but I never ever came first. I had an 'I'm tired, I'm tired' song that I used to sing off-key to the refrain from the nursery rhyme 'Ring-a-ring-a-rosy' every morning before school. I would sit sulking on Dor's bed with Mavie brushing and plaiting my hair ('the *bladdie pennetjies'),* all puffy lips and irritation and just as *bladdie* tired as me, no doubt.

After the hair, I would be inspected to see that the pleated navy skirt was put on straight, the white shirt tucked in and the narrow red tie pulled all the way up and not hanging loose, the navy jersey buttoned correctly, the white socks neatly folded and the black Harley Street T-bar shoes buckled in the right hole.

Ivan polished my shoes when he polished his in the evening. They were polished right down to the soles. 'People would think badly of you if the soles weren't polished,' he used to say.

Oh man, where's your head? I might have responded. We were all thought of badly in this country, from the moment we were born, because of our skin colour.

Lastly, the white Panama hat with the red ribbon around the brim would be jammed on my head. In winter, the white socks and hat were replaced with knee-high grey socks and a black beret that was too big for my head.

From the age of five in 1967, I would be marched up Heather-ley Road and commanded to look left and right before crossing the road to bus stop 12 outside Niefies Shop. There Mavie and I would wait for sisters Natalie and Glynnis Quimpo who were in Standards five and four respectively. They would escort me on the bus journey and long walk up the lane between St Ignatius Catholic Church and the block of shops and flats next to the school. I would be deposited at the door of the dreaded Sub A class.

Travelling to school on the double-decker Tramways bus that looked like pictures of London's red buses was my first encounter with apartheid-era segregation. We weren't allowed to sit downstairs but were harried upstairs, where it was filled to capacity. The downstairs seating that was reserved for white people was always less crowded.

Travelling to and from Claremont by bus was frightening. The bus had no doors. You jumped on at the back and climbed the steps to the upper deck.

Navigating the downward journey was a daily nightmare. I was petrified that I would fall down the stairs and shoot right out the opening while the bus was moving and then be crushed by the cars tailgating the bus. I'd seen women fall out the bus several times. They'd never been crushed but I felt sorry for them, imagining the embarrassment of taking a tumble in public.

Just like on the trains today, men stood at that opening, clinging to the pole on the entrance landing. The buses had conductors back then, but there came a time on the single-decker buses when it was just a driver-conductor.

Mavie would come to school to fetch me at noon, until the Sub A teacher, Miss Morris, said it wasn't necessary anymore. Miss Morris promised to stand with the children at the bus stop outside Villager's Rugby Club sports field and see them safely onto the Lansdowne bus. Many travelled to Wetton and one child went as far as Crossroads, where there was a thriving coloured community before the Old Crossroads squatter area grew out from under the Port Jackson trees.

Added to my anxieties was the constant panic about losing my bus fare. The stormwater grill at the bus stop was a place to fear: stuff could get lost down there.

One winter's day, I got on the bus and could not find my two cents coin. I knew I'd had it when I left school, but it had vanished. The bus driver waited patiently and the more he waited, the more anxious I became until a kind lady sitting in the front seat got up to pay the fare. She must have been white because the front rows of the single-decker buses were reserved for whites and everybody else had to move to the back. The irony was that most of the time you couldn't tell who was white and who was not. I said thank you to the woman like I had been drilled to say.

The rest of the journey was a haze of the usual worry about missing my bus stop. Once I nearly missed the stop as I struggled to push past the crowd to the front of the bus to get off. I managed to jump out as the bus was pulling away. No broken bones, fortunately.

I was always relieved to be back on familiar territory. There was Laubscher's farm and, on the other side of the road, the surgery where Dor worked.

Mavie would be waiting for me. We crossed the field, which flooded in winter, to Dale Street. I always admired the berry bushes that grew wild next to the Petersen's house and clumps of snowdrops and arum lilies. When the latter popped up, you knew we were right in the heart of winter.

Mavie cross-examined me about my day on this walk and I was learning to give a good account of my school experiences. I told her that day that I'd lost my bus fare and that a kind lady helped me. I was expecting a *skelling* for being *kens*, but . . . silence!

Maybe Mavie was just glad that I arrived home safely. That year a little girl had gone missing from where she played outside Lee-Pan's shop on Lansdowne Road. Her disappearance left in its wake a communal shock, fear and finally sadness. Every day, as soon as I stepped out of our yard, I felt afraid. The five-year-old girl, who'd had the same surname as mine[5] though we weren't related, was all I could think of. I seem to recall her name was Faiza and she lived in a wood and iron house in the Chinese neighbours' backyard. Her mother's name was Dinah.

The police searched everywhere for Faiza, questioning the neighbours and even looking through our gardens. After a lengthy search, they found her little body near the canal on Turfhall Road. The council was only just starting to build Hanover Park

---

5   Concerning the Davids surname: In about 186 years of slavery at the Cape, slaves were captured in their homelands from many places in the Indian Ocean, West and East Africa and shipped to Cape Town. They were stripped of everything they owned, including their names. They were assigned new ones using days of the week, months, and names of emperors, gods and mythical figures. Do the names Januarie, Februarie, October, Apollos, Alexander, Kupido, Hector, Adonis and Titus sound familiar? Often names were taken from the Old Testament: Adam, Abraham, Jacob, Isaac, Samuel, Solomon and David, among others. When such a slave had a child, an S was added to the father's name and the child would become Davids, Solomons, Samuels, and so on. Some names were based on the name of the man who fathered the child, such as Hendricks, Pieters, etc. There were more male than female slaves at the Cape, numbering at least 4:1. Because slaves were a commodity, they could not marry, they could not own property, they could not choose where they lived or who they worked for. Their production and reproduction were strictly controlled and recorded, and they had no right to their own children, among many other limitations.

   Van Rensburg, A. *Let them Speak – Slave Stamouers of South Africa*. South Africa's Stamouers. https://www.stamouers.com/people-of-south-africa/slaves/674-let-them-speak-slave-stamouers-of-south-africa. Last accessed 04/03/2020.

at the time. Later in court, it emerged that she'd been lured away with sweets by a just-released convict called Chookoo.

I don't know what terrible deeds he did to her before he strangled her, because I was not privy to that information. After the court case, Dinah and her family moved away, broken by sadness.

After Faiza's death the usual, ever-present threat and danger grew even bigger in my mind. My elders repeated – again – the rule that I was not to talk to strangers and ever take anything that was offered to me by one.

Mavie and I walked home in silence. I dumped my book case on the floor and went to wash my hands as was expected of me. Then I made for the chair in the corner by the window where I could look out over the garden.

I usually sat in that spot to eat my lunch at the small table where meal preparations were done as it was right near the stove. Mavie's always-tuned-in-transistor radio sat on the table, next to a stainless-steel kettle. When I graduated to doing homework, my lunch spot became one of many workspaces.

I munched my cheese-and-tomato sandwich and drank my tea, looking forward to the plain Simba chips that Mavie bought for me as a treat. She was bustling about as usual, but on her way to the fridge behind me, she zapped off my beret which I had failed to remove.

'Oh, my word, look what I found!' she exclaimed, trying hard not to laugh.

Alarm bells! It had to be lice, my other new dread since starting school.

She opened her hand and there was the two-cent coin. When she saw the look on my face, she cracked up completely. I'd put the coin under my beret for safekeeping and then forgotten about it. Mavie dined out on that story for a long time.

Quite apart from the daunting commute, school meant coming to terms with one's sins. The first time I heard about original sin, I thought deeply about this matter and concluded that the soul looked like a pomegranate pip with a black spot where a worm had burrowed through the red, juicy fruit.

I learnt about the inner workings of sin in catechism class. During the first two years of school, catechism prepared junior Catholics for the sacraments and the First Holy Communion. We were taught about confession and how before we could receive communion, our confessions would be heard by the priests. It must have been quite exciting for the priests to hear the sins of lots of little seven-year-olds.

The aim, we gleaned, was not to die before you reached initiation into the crucial sacrament of Holy Communion, otherwise you were going to stew for a long time in purgatory. Besides catechism every day, once a week each grade or standard had a designated day for attending mass at the church next to the school.

Prone to death rattling bouts of tonsillitis, it looked to me like I wasn't going to make it to my First Holy Communion. I would die of my illnesses and my snotty nose before then, on a one-way ticket to purgatory.

I had difficulty swallowing because my uvula was extra-long and blocked the passageway to my throat. My tonsils were always swollen and inflamed. In my first year of school, I had an operation to remove my tonsils and part of the uvula at Somerset Hospital. I had the time of my life eating jelly and ice-cream. Unfortunately, I didn't have much of a break from the torment of school because the operation had been scheduled just before the school holidays.

It was during that time that I entered a parallel life of learning. School was one thing, but it was my second life of learning that sustained me: I was taught how to make things with my hands.

Everybody I knew made things. Perhaps they harboured dreams of earning a living from their handiwork, an unspoken longing for independence and freedom.

In Claremont, Granny Davids crocheted and sewed anything from cloths to bedspreads and clothing. She used to buy her crochet cotton, wool and material at Brenners Clothing and Haberdashery which was opposite Livingstone High School.

Ivan's eldest sister, Aunty Doreen, was a teacher and an amateur actress who also did dressmaking and crocheting. She used patterns from the German *Burda* magazine for her clothes. His middle sister, Aunty Edna, made tailored costumes and perfect wedding gowns with beading, and his youngest sister, Aunty Auriel, sewed, crocheted and knitted garments.

Ivan's brothers made and played things too. Uncle Cyril built stereo systems, did woodwork and metalwork and played the clarinet. Uncle Charles painted in oils. Uncle Lennon made exquisite wooden jewellery boxes. Uncle Julian played the guitar. Uncle Robert was a multi-instrumental jazz musician and composed musicals. He also invented games. Uncle Stanley was a graphic designer and made clocks from exotic woods. He played the saxophone and flute.

My father Ivan drew in pen, pencil, charcoal and chalk pastels, painted in oils, sculpted in clay, carved in driftwood and made linocut prints.

After his season on the whaling vessel *Willem Barends*, he painted miniature Bruegel-like scenes of life in the South Atlantic. For these, he used a piece of already clean and dried out whale

91

bone of 40 cm by 30 cm, two whale teeth and two pieces of cartilage. These were anchored on a thick piece of wood and the whole presented as a sculpture.

He also painted big scenes on pieces of primed board of little male figures cutting whales on the boat. With sharp pieces of ice jutting out of the vastness of the ocean the scenes looked cold and miserable. The paintings were part of his one and only art exhibition, held in 1968 in a building at the junction of Sir Lowry Road and Darling Street when parts of District Six still stood. I don't own any of my father's paintings. Most of them were sold to extended family members and friends. Or they were given away. Years later, I saw a painting he made in the 1970s at a family friend's house in London.

In those years, the Cape Town artist Erik Laubscher, who helped Ivan with his exhibition, and many others in his circle who were on the brink of fame, often made their way to our backdoor. From there they went to the lounge to talk. They spoke of the magic of modern art and how things should loosen up. The latest art manuals were discussed in reverent tones and Ivan's latest works admired.

Ivan served them tea in fine porcelain English cups, delivered on a tray with a doily, a plate of cookies and the obligatory cake plates. Ivan might not have believed in Jesus, but he certainly believed in the art of tea.

He used to save my eccentric drawings. These gave my Sub B teacher Mrs Newman headaches, especially the one of Jesus wearing an astronaut suit on his ascent into heaven. I was always informed of the latest world news and was shown newspaper pictures, so the astronaut idea must have come to me during the space race. In another picture, made just before Easter break,

Ivan's Impressionist painting of a backyard dwelling on Lee-Pan's property, 1970s.

Jesus wore a purple cat-suit on the cross. It was after all the time of the hippies.

Ivan's artist friends nodded over the drawings and peered at me as though I were an alien specimen. They spoke about the drawings in the strange codes of artists and I would eventually slip away to the yard for playtime.

Ivan knew lots of artists and sometimes he and his friend Basil Chandler used to paint en plein in Wynberg Park or outside in our yard or garden. They both turned out brilliant paintings. Art fashion at the time, however, was that the modern should be embraced, and so by the end of the 1960s, their work had veered away from the precise Old Dutch masters' style they had been taught, towards abstraction and semi-abstraction.

Stella's boyfriend Meneer Wilfie was an avid photographer, but neither Ivan nor he shared their particular crafts with me.

Even though I was encouraged to use my hands, the collective will of my elders was that I had to get an education. Change and upliftment must come for the next generation, was the message hidden behind often stern expressions. I took this very seriously. I knew I had an obligation to do well at school, even though I didn't like it.

Mavie was sympathetic. Sometimes she let me get away with feeling-too-sick-for-school. Outright *bladdie* lies.

'I hated school too,' she confessed. 'I used to think that it was a place where you couldn't breathe. I spent most of Sub A out of school.' This was about the same time Grandpa José was working at his after-retirement job as a night watchman at Sans Souci Estate. 'I'd walk to Claremont with Stella and we'd arrive there about the same time Grandpa would be going home. Then I would turn right around and go home with him. I spent the whole of Sub A learning Portuguese letters and numbers and speaking Portuguese. I repeated Sub A the next year. Old Jack used to drive us to school to make sure that I went.'

Only as an adult did I learn that not being able to breathe signalled the onset of an anxiety attack. Mavie suffered from debilitating anxiety, but it remained undiagnosed her whole life.

After Mavie was done regaling me with her past misadventures, she donned her stern expression again and gave me her go-to-school motivation speech: 'If you fail, you will have to go work in the fish factory at the little bridge.' She was referring to the fish canning factory in Rosedon Road, opposite Our Lady Help of Christians Catholic Church.

That was a fate too ghastly to contemplate, so I did my best at school. And in the afternoons, when the bus driver revved over the gut-dropping little bridge that crossed the canal that separated Claremont from Lansdowne, I looked everywhere but at the fish factory. If the fish factory workers were on the bus and somebody stared at them, they would *skel* that person. I didn't fancy a *skelling* because I got a lot of that at home.

In the afternoons, I would do homework and then play outside. In the evenings after supper, the aunties taught me crafts beside the woodstove. Skeins of wool or yarn came in lengths that were loosely coiled and knotted. Dor would loop the skein over her wrists and I would roll balls of wool. That is where I started working with wool.

After that, she taught me the art of casting on and off, and of knitting plain and purl, then making cables or frilly patterns. She taught me to read patterns, make buttonholes, shape sleeves and armholes, knit ribbing, bands and collars, and using a darning needle and wool thread to stitch all the parts of a garment together. I learnt to make pompoms for caps and button loops for garments.

By the time I was seven I'd already mastered the art of knitting a baby's matinée set from cap to jacket to booties for my eldest cousin Joline's baby son, Mark.

I knitted the matinée set just in time because soon after that I tripped and broke my arm while I delivered a dish and eggs to Mrs Neethling across Heatherley Road. She was making a Marie Biscuit tart for Mavie, who had already delivered the dry ingredients. Fearful of a *skelling* if I let go of the expensive Pyrex dish, I held on and fell awkwardly. Afterwards, I went home and resumed play. Only later that Saturday did someone notice my right arm was swollen and that I wasn't using it. I was taken to Somerset Hospital, where I had to have an operation. The arm was not put into plaster of Paris, just a sling. The happiest outcome was that I was off school for a few days!

By now I was in Standard 1. Staying home for the entire predicted six weeks' recovery period was not an option. The school principal, Mr McGowan, arranged to collect me in the mornings in his pristine white Valiant with its black vinyl top. He'd lift the other children in our road too if they happened to be on their way to the bus stop. Being unable to write at school meant I had to memorise everything.

Knitting and playing were temporarily on hold until my arm mended completely, but I was soon back up and running – and making things.

We were taught needlecraft at school and I started embroidery. Stella taught me to embroider just outlines, not the fancy, delicately coloured pictures in beautiful embroidery cottons which were her forte. Her work was exquisite but she didn't sell her cloths and aprons. What she didn't keep, she would present as gifts to friends and family. Embroidery is an expensive craft and I did it only for a short time.

One day, I was hanging around with Aunty Dorothy, Uncle Joey's wife, and she taught me how to crochet chains and patterns. I acquired a crochet hook from somewhere and soon progressed to making caps and ponchos.

I think Aunty Dorothy took pity on me because for most of that year my mom had been in and out of hospital due to a difficult pregnancy as a result of diabetes. She would be away from home for weeks at a time. I stayed after school at Aunty Dorothy's house, wedged between Lennie's Barber Shop and Shiba's Shoe Store on Lansdowne Road. One of the aunties would collect me in the late afternoon.

One day Aunty Dorothy asked, 'What is that on your legs?'

I'd been playing in the courtyard with her granddaughter Lee-Lee and her friend Waaskie from 3 Dale Road. Both were younger than me.

I looked at her blankly and she came closer to have a look. 'They're bruises! Where did you get that? Who hit you?'

Across my legs were at least six blue marks where Miss Assam had hit me with a cane that day. I was in Standard 2 then. I'd zoned out as she hit me, concentrating on not crying in front of my classmates. She was caning me because she thought that the dry skin on the back of my head was lice. Stella had not had time to wash my hair at the weekend with the special shampoo used for it and by midweek the dried skin showed.

Aunty Dorothy was outraged and when Stella came to fetch me, she insisted that she report it to the principal. Before work the next day, Stella went to see Mr McGowan, who was quite apologetic. Miss Assam was cross-examined and made to apologise. They said they did not know about the difficulties at home. I hadn't told them.

The next day at assembly they prayed for Mavie. Mr McGowan informed the Irish parish priest at Our Lady Help of Christians, Father Donaghy, about Mavie's illness. He came around to visit and to his surprise found a lounge full of floral arrangements. His visit coincided with the first church flower arranger from church emigrating to Australia and Dor was co-opted to take over the duties she would fulfil for the next 30 years.

During weekdays, she worked as a receptionist at the surgery, and every Saturday afternoon as the church's flower arranger. She also did arrangements before big feast days, weddings, funerals and formal dances.

Church had always been a big part of our family's life. Its

seasons and traditions that go back hundreds of years provided solidity. It was like nature providing the guavas, loquats, apples and pears in winter, and all the rest in summer. It was predictable and steadfast.

Mavie's pregnancy ended in sadness. The doctors were unable to keep my sister Antonia alive. She was a micro-cephalic, born with her brains in a sac outside her skull, and she only lived two days, long enough to be baptised by Father Donaghy.

Only Ivan, Dor, Stella and Father Donaghy saw my baby sister in ICU. Mavie never saw her, nor was she able to attend the funeral. I prayed like anything to keep my mother alive. It was touch and go for her. It must have been very depressing to end up a chronic diabetic with high blood pressure at the age of 32. No one ever explained to her that stress aggravated diabetes.

As a child, I got the sense that all the 'nice' people we knew were intolerant towards illnesses in others. There was often talk of it being 'all in the mind' and somehow the ill person seemed to be in the wrong. They were not trying hard enough and were lazy, was the subtext. I imagine all this judgement compounded stress, which made physical illness worse. Ironically, these same 'nice' people turned into complete drama queens when they were afflicted by chronic conditions later in life.

Mavie's failing health was not the only problem at home. As young as I was, I knew Ivan was not playing by the rules. Into my fourth year of catechism, I had a strong sense of right and wrong. More than once, I'd hear him tell women that Mavie was dying as an opening gambit, a ham-handed attempt at signalling that it was okay to flirt.

Nothing ever happened. It was all in his mind, a kind of opportunism. I saw him charm and flirt and imply and it gave me a bad feeling.

Everywhere I looked around me, I was not getting a good impression of people. It stood me in good stead, though, as it quickened the onset of discernment. If I were Mavie and Dor, I wouldn't have aimed so hard to please society.

Stella would never have taken that bit of advice from me if I were to give it because she was too far gone down the rabbit hole with Meneer Wilfie, the king of bad manners. He had a bad reputation with regard to his temperament – and it wasn't undeserved.

It was around this time that it dawned on me that people were silly enough to consider faking happiness and *joie de vivre* as essentials to navigating life. I nurtured a different way of living and understood the benefits of keeping busy and creating things in times of extreme stress and sadness.

I kept going with the crocheting Aunty Dorothy taught me. Every time I went down the road with Dor during her lunch hour to Shoprite (where Osman's is today), she bought me balls of yarn from Half Price Store. I made garments with colourful, abstract patterns. I mixed contrasting colours, either rolling two colours together into a ball of wool or using different colours in the patterns I made.

It was 1970, the time of the hippies, and my pile of children's caps and ponchos grew while the designs burgeoned in eccentricity and colour. One day Miss Mary Andrews, a family friend, said she would sell my creations at the clothing factory in Woodstock where she was a supervisor. She had been given her Group Areas removals notice and had to find a temporary home before emigrating to England, so she stayed with us for about a year.

My first batch sold out in a week. I kept on getting more orders until Miss Mary set sail and my sales avenue closed.

From all the left-over balls of wool, I crocheted colourful squares which were set aside until I had enough to stitch them into a psychedelic-looking afghan.

Stella did a lot of shopping – placebo buying, as I think of it – to be happy. Sometimes I would help her build puzzles. She was the family's chief player of cards, rings, board games and dominoes. She didn't teach me those games, but we did play Monopoly. Sometimes the neighbours would join in for round after round of the game. It did my small heart proud that I could beat the teenagers and the older people at their game.

An interest in handicrafts was not unique to my family. Next door, Mrs Henry's son Richie made tie-dyed hippie t-shirts and did glass-blowing in the yard. He came up with all sorts of colourful shapes that were used for ashtrays. I longed for a tie-dyed hippie t-shirt, especially one made from a grandpa vest with three buttons down the front, but Mavie nixed that idea. No hippie clothes, no ways!

Richie taught us *laaities* how to make our kites, using the cane bamboo from our yard, fishing gut and soft, colourful, shiny sheets of tissue paper from Lee-Pan's shop on the corner. If we did not have any cents to spend on tissue paper, we made kites from old newspapers and string, but those dive-bombed quickly.

Mrs Henry made patchwork quilts – what quilters call crazy quilts – and utility bags from her family's old clothes. All those colours were mesmerising. I wanted to learn to make the same colours in paint, but Ivan cut me off from doing too much art. I was limited to crayons, pencils and Koki pens. I was never allowed to dip into the watercolour pans or the oil pastels or the soft chalk pastels that he had but never used. And while he taught my older cousins to shade and shape forms, he never extended his lessons to me.

As early as my primary school years he began to transform me into a head-over-hands person, pushing and priming, the way all adults seem to do with the next generation, towards professions so we could have better lives. Many years later, after false starts in two other professions, I would become a journalist.

But I always remained baffled about what constituted 'better lives', and who decides this?

If music be

IN SPITE OF the country's politics and psychosis, life went on for us.

The arts, and especially music, played an enormous part in consoling hurting souls and broken hearts. People walked around heavy and sorely put upon, but to acknowledge it out loud would be like handing over power to this entity called apartheid.

Weekdays were reserved for dealing with the authorities and the dilemmas and crises they caused. Weekends everyone took a breath. If people weren't spending time outdoors, they created celebrations or entertainment in their communities, usually centred around whatever church they attended. There would be concerts throughout the year and bazaars in December.

And everywhere there were traditional ballroom dances for those who loved a twirl on the dance floor. Carefully painted ladies would dress to the nines in long lurex evening gowns, metallic coloured stilettos, fake fur and paste jewellery, glass beads made to look like diamonds and rubies. They carried platters of snacks to the events and the men, dressed up in evening suits and bowties, brought along their own booze. This tradition is still alive and well and thriving on the Cape Flats.

Band members were treated like celebs. For all that they brought great joy through their music, musicians who chose to ply their trade professionally endured harsh rejection under the apartheid laws. They were not allowed to perform for white audiences or at venues in white areas like at the big theatres. Those who did manage to get gigs playing in an orchestra for a dance show, for instance, were hidden from view so that the whites could not see them.

The celebrated jazz pianist Tony Schilder, a schoolmate of Mavie's and Ivan's from Livingstone High, told their friend Elsa how he played the piano for the stripper Glenda Kemp who used the pet python *Oupa* in her dance repertoire.

Ms Kemp shocked the Calvinistic Afrikaner community when she dared to bare all before audiences, slap-bang in the middle of the *verkrampte* 1970s. *Skandelik!* There were always stories on the back pages of the *Sunday Times* and *Rapport* – the sex, sin, skinner and scandal pages – on Ms Kemp's latest escapades with the python or her run-ins with the authorities. She, with *Oupa* draped around her shoulders, wiggled in defiant nakedness before the altar of authoritarianism and the two of them were arrested several times on charges of public indecency. Kemp persevered, pushing at boundaries with the fortitude of an activist and for this she garnered a huge following of fans among liberals.

'Tony,' Elsa reported in a whisper, 'had to sit behind a curtain to play the piano. Just so that he, a coloured man, could not see a naked white woman dance. He was given cues by the stage-hands when to change tempo.'

And there was the story of classical pianist Reggie Dreyer who in 1960 auditioned and was accepted to play as a concert pianist with the Cape Town Symphony Orchestra. On the eve of his debut, where he was due to play Mozart's Piano Concerto No 23 in A: K488, the apartheid authorities cancelled his performance.

Mr Dreyer became a music teacher instead and excelled at being a church organist and choirmaster, as well as a classical and jazz musician. He created many other musical projects for himself, until 57 years later when he finally made his debut with the Cape Town Symphony Orchestra at Artscape, playing the very piece he'd been banned from playing all those years ago.

When I visited him at home in Retreat in 2017 to report on his story for the *Cape Argus*, he told me, 'It was a disappointing time in my life. It wasn't a good thing, but you don't go and sit, moaning and groaning and blaming it all on apartheid. I had to get on with my life. There was so much to do. I just wanted to play.'

Many musicians had that attitude: they just wanted to play, no matter the seemingly insurmountable obstacles apartheid laws placed in their path. And they did. Ivan's jazz musician brother Robert, along with his friends such as jazz guitarist and big band leader Darryl Andrews, took to the road and went to play in big bands at resorts in neighbouring countries. The most popular of these were in Lesotho and Swaziland, where the audiences were mostly white South Africans, letting their hair down before returning to their buttoned-up lives back home.

All musicians had tales to tell of record deals gone sour. Some record labels pressurised them into changing their songs so as not to raise the ire of the authorities and radios didn't give them enough airplay for them to get big hits. Often, if they managed to record, they didn't own copyright on their creations and were robbed of earning royalties. Many musicians became iconic figures, playing in nightclubs and other venues in coloured areas, and some are still kicking around in coloured areas. Others went overseas where they were celebrated for their compositions and their achievements.

If the 1960s had a soundtrack in my mind, it would not be Elvis, Cliff Richards, the Beatles or Stella's collection of Percy Sledge seven-singles. But it would also not be the old men gathered at our house and singing 'Auld Lang Syne' and 'I'll be seeing you'. No, it would be the sound of opera.

I heard *Va Pensiero* (the Hebrew slave chorus from Verdi's *Nabucco*) for the first time after a mad trot to keep up with Mavie down Lansdowne Road. We went over the railway bridge to Lansdowne Civic Centre Hall to attend a matinee classical concert performed by the music pupils of Livingstone High.

Mavie had just heard about the concert that morning, acquired tickets and hijacked me as soon as I got off at bus stop 12 from an excruciatingly hard morning of being in Sub A. She hurried me through a snack and denied me the usual afternoon activity of climbing trees. And, to my embarrassment, she sent my chommies packing when they turned up to play. She had more important things for me to do: receive my introduction to 'serious' music.

The concert shocked me out of the trees I didn't get to climb that day. Those teenagers played the violin, piano and flute. They sang arias and choruses and the school anthem which I would learn seven years later when I went to Livingstone High myself. But it was *Va Pensiero* that stuck for years after, although I only learned its title in the 1990s.

The translation from Italian says, 'Go, thoughts, on golden wings; go, settle upon the slopes and hills, where warm and soft and fragrant are the breezes of our sweet native land!' How appropriate for a time when people were losing their land all around us.

Mavie went home starry-eyed. She convinced as many people

as possible that they just *had* to attend the concert. She contacted her ticket supplier and went back for the following evening's performance with Ivan and a few friends in tow.

Soon after, Stella bought two LPs of the concert that some Livingstone kids were selling for school funds. Mavie played the blitz out of that LP, the only one she ever owned.

Opera was her thing and her ally was Mrs Janap Daniels, our Heatherley Road opposite neighbour, who was a seamstress with CAPAB before the Nico Malan Theatre, now called the Artscape, was built. Mrs Janap would take Mavie, Ivan and Mrs Atta with her to attend the Capab Opera dress rehearsals, at the Alhambra Theatre. Mrs Janap's husband, Mr Salie Daniels, was not interested in opera. He only liked the Malay *koorliedjies* and *moppies,* which he went all the way to the Bo Kaap to enjoy.

Mavie and Ivan lapped up every note, endlessly grateful for Mrs Janap's thoughtfulness in taking them along. Apartheid laws excluded them from attending the CAPAB opera. The working people who put their all into making props and outfits, and were involved in other crucial preparations for the big shows, were excluded from the big opening night, but dressed up in formal evening wear to attend the dress rehearsal because that was the thing to do: you dressed up for the opera, ballroom dances, weddings and funerals and anything else that called for a chance to don your best finery. And you shone. The dress rehearsal included a glossy programme and the audience was mixed.

Among the operas they saw were Giuseppe Verdi's *La Traviata* and *Rigoletto.*

By the 1970s they heard about the Eon Group's variety concerts, so that's what Mavie saved for in her entertainment fund.

At the Joseph Stone Auditorium in Athlone we saw a white CAPAB production of Giacomo Puccini's *Madame Butterfly*. We could not see them in 'their' theatre, so they came to perform for us in Athlone. We also saw an Eon Group production of Georges Bizet's *Carmen*.

And it is Bizet's *March of The Toreadors* that sounds most like the early 1970s to me.

From 1973 onwards, we didn't see any full-length opera. If there was a variety concert at Savio Hall at our church or the Luxurama Theatre in Wynberg, there would usually be an opera singer included, singing arias. Sometimes we went to the Joseph Stone to see British movies, like the *Carry on* and *Hayley Mills* movies. And sometimes there would be showings of Italian movies, with subtitles, featuring Sophia Loren.

I realise now that the increase in entertainment, whether in the form of variety concerts or movies, came as greater pressure was applied by the forced removals and demolitions happening throughout the city.

Ivan's brother Robert wrote two musicals, so we went to see his shows when those were staged at Lansdowne Civic Centre. It was said to have been shut down by the cops for provocative content and anti-apartheid lines in the speaking parts and in lyrics. Both musicals dealt with forced removals and resettlement. Who knew what would cause the authorities to react, and when?

Mavie used to say, 'Beautiful music takes me far away.' At the end of her life, when music kept her going, Franz Lehar's *Dein ist Mein Ganzes Herz,* from the 1929 opera *Land of Smiles*, as sung by Placido Domingo claimed top spot as her favourite aria. It must have been like that for many people in those harrowing years. Music flew them to higher ground, far away from the madness of the rulers.

At home there was always music via the hum of Springbok radio or Stella's record collection – something would arrest the ears for a short while before the attention moved on again.

I was everybody's companion of choice when nobody closer to their own age was around, thus Stella would haul me all the way to the Gem Bioscope in Woodstock. We had to endure four bus changes to watch Elvis films, and to this day Elvis scares the living daylights out of me. (At least three decades later I was to see the places where many of the scenes for his movie *Blue Hawaii* were shot on the island of Oahu.)

Closer to home, my teenage cousins Marlene and Lorna from Bridgetown, who used to babysit me during their school holidays, would take me along to the Broadway Bioscope on Lansdowne Road, fondly referred to as the Bug House. We would see matinee showings of the Beatles films.

I knew the Beatles songs, just like I knew Cliff Richard's old 'Going on a Summer holiday', from watching my two oldest girl cousins Joline and Flo-Anne practising the twist in their kitchen at home, dolled up to the nines in their tights, fitted tops and the pumps that had just made it onto the fashion scene. Ever since, I keep a safe distance from sixties music. Overload, I think.

The Broadway Bioscope, by the way, now houses a Pakistani barber, an Islamic fashion boutique and a café, while upstairs there is an entertainment hall called The Venue.

Every song from 'The Sound of Music' and 'My Fair Lady' was taken to heart in some quarters of our community, and were done to death at variety concerts.

Just before my primary school days ended, Stella took me to a local show with Richard John Smith, Jonathan Butler and Ronnie Joyce at the Luxurama. She was a firm supporter of 'local is lekker'. (She even backed the Springboks when everybody else backed the opposing teams, like New Zealand, France or England.) She didn't take me with to see her favourites though: Percy Sledge and Lovelace Watkins, nor to see her friend, local singer Verushka from Wynberg. Meneer Wilfie accompanied her on those occasions.

I think we cloaked ourselves in music as a protective layer of warmth against the cold, harsh realities of life in those years. Music was apotropaic to ward off evil – something like strings of garlic hung at windows or bags of salt put in their cupboards. It didn't work very well. The trucks and bulldozers still rolled in to chase and bundle up and break down. Our community's 'many-splendoured' lives and times scraped to the edges of white South Africa in pursuit of unattainable neatness and uniformity.

And life went on. Life is like that. Obstacle placed in your path? No fear. Become fluid. Flow around it. Soon the obstacle will be a thing of the past as you flow on toward the coast, a point of departure. And there were more than enough departures. Departures from the past, departures for England, Australia, Canada, New Zealand and Europe. Departures from home.

At house parties, even ones where no booze was allowed, like at our place, there would be much excitement and joy with chatting, plates to fill with delicious snacks or finger suppers, and whatever there was to drink. Somebody would haul out the records and play Victor Silvester or Mrs Mills dance music and the dancers would be out there on the floor showing their skill. Sometimes they'd even dance the square.

But as the evening wore on, and especially if the party was in honour of family or friends leaving to find freedom overseas, the sadness could be sensed. Even the laughter had a melancholy ring to it.

At our home, some old sentimental man, usually Mr Henry from next door or Grandpa Jack's Cousin Wilfred (who went everywhere with his lovely, quiet wife Aunty Katie and his mistress Minnie in tow), would always end the evening with renditions of *Auld Lang Syne* and Billy Holliday's *'I'll be seeing you'*.

Grandpa Jack sometimes came with Miss Lizzie, Miss Audrey and her son Gregory, like Athlone royalty in the black-and-white Zephyr with its flashy fins. Uncle Joey and Uncle Kenny and their families also came to the parties, when they had nothing else to do.

'I'll be seeing you in all the old familiar places / that my heart embraces all day through,' and so it would go on. If I knew the original Billie Holiday song, or if Cassandra Wilson or Diana Krall had been around back then, I would have preferred their versions, because the unsaid in the old men singing off-key was unbearable, in the way barely expressed raw emotion always is. And to crown it all the old women would join in too.

Sorry, but all that positive-thinking talk – put a smile on it and soldier on, you will attract wealth – just didn't cut it when life was a hastily scribbled signature away from broken dreams and aspirations, a click away from homelessness and hopelessness.

The gatherings at home weren't always parties. Sometimes Meneer Wilfie had slides evenings of his and Stella's travels to London and the Continent, or with pictures of local scenery or of blooms taken in the garden. And everybody would be on tenterhooks in case it was one of his off-key moody and snapping days. Lots of people had projectors and would show movies at their homes. As always, there would be eats.

We could only try, right? Better to sing that song, dance that dance, play music or show that movie or pictures all the time.

And pray fervently to get through that tunnel of darkness unscathed.

There were fairs and merry-go-rounds to attend. Close to home, on Lansdowne Road there stood Laubscher's farm (Islamia's campus today) where there was a beautiful hedge of pink primroses at the entranceway with its wooden gate that always stood open. In winter, the land would flood in places, a clear indication that the area was part of the Cape Flats aquifer.

In summer in the field next to the farm caravans of exotic-looking people, dressed like what was known as 'gypsies' back then, would bring us a merry-go-round fair, all under the watchful gaze of ducks, cows, a horse and an assortment of barnyard animals in the adjoining field.

It was the only kind of fair I ever went to. Mavie usually took me in the afternoon. Those pretty horses going round and round were seriously cool. I never got to go on the ever-popular scare-monger though. I was too young. From our kitchen, we heard teen girls screaming their heads off on their dive-bomber escapades, feigning damsel-in-distress for their particular brand of leading men.

I never went to the Mardi Gras in Wynberg nor to the one at City Park Stadium in Athlone. I saw the UCT Rag Day parade only once. I saw the Christmas lights in Adderley Street and Somerset West Main Road. But I never saw The Coon Carnival, as it was called then (it's now called the Cape Town Minstrel Carnival), on Tweede Nuwe Jaar in the city centre.

In our area, one of the troupe – Kaapse Klopse in all their finery – from Harfield Village would pass by on their march further down Lansdowne Road. The Atchars, they were called, scary painted characters who lunged at the little kids, choppers in hand.

Sometimes string bands marched by, especially around Christmas. One band would always stop to play outside the opposite neighbour's house. Stella adored them. And then, throughout the year, the brigade and drum majorettes from All Saints Anglican Church would also pass our house. The church celebrated the centenary of its building in Denver Road in 2018.

The Talfalah School band from Claremont sometimes marched down Lansdowne Road dressed in green tartan kilts with all its various accoutrements. Many years later, at the World Expo 92 in Seville, Spain, I watched an outdoor performance of the Royal Jordanian Armed Forces band, and their sound and the green tartan headgear reminded me of Talfalah.

The parades drew young and old outside to watch and there was a sense of occasion about them.

Early December meant going to all the church bazaars in the area, starting with Our Lady Help of Christians Catholic Church and All Saints Anglican Church. There was fudge, coconut ice, pink *ghoemahare* – the ubiquitous candy floss of bazaars, fetes and fairs the world over – and gooey toffee apples. There were handmade gifts, variety performances and donkey rides for the little ones. Everybody turned up to support bazaar day, to eat themselves silly and do some gift-buying for Christmas. I had a major stash of childhood treasures acquired at those bazaars, including a Pears' Cyclopaedia, a gift from our kind priest Father Donaghy who came from Londonderry, Northern Ireland.

At the Catholic churches, the congregations were always racially mixed because the church refused to bow down to apartheid's segregation laws. There was a place for everyone and every person had his or her duties. They greeted one another, sat next to one another, worshipped together and served in the same church organisations, like the choir, the church bazaar and the various prayer groups. The congregants went to the movies at Savio Hall on Sunday evenings or to variety shows, especially the Saint Patrick's Day shows, so popular because of the Irish clergy. The priests, there could be as many as ten of them, would sing Irish songs. We saw *Lord of the Dance* moves before it became a worldwide phenomenon in the 1990s.

Opera was Mavie's favourite music, but she also enjoyed travelling by train on the Cape Flats line for two stations to reach the Kismet in Athlone to attend musical films. The first time we went, we saw *Hoor my Lied,* an Afrikaans musical drama, of which I understood very little, since I was only five, though I did enjoy the garden scenes. The last two we saw, just before our lives changed completely, were *Saturday Night Fever* and *Grease.* My mother had graduated from a fan of the Afrikaans crooner Gé Korsten to a full-on John Travolta enthusiast.

'Oh, oh, oh, staying alive, staying alive . . .'

In my early teens, I was too naive to grasp the irony.

Exhale city, breathe in country

MY ENTIRE FAMILY had always been fond of outings to see the views. These trips became more intense as our neighbourhood emptied of renters who'd been dispatched to newly constructed places in Hanover Park and elsewhere. Around the mountains we went, either with Ivan in his little blue Morris Minor when he wasn't working weekends, or with the neighbours. Always the adults said, 'We will never leave this city, look at this beauty.'

And yet the very nature of these outings was that they were steeped in the thought of leaving. We spent a lot of time seeing friends off at the Cape Town Harbour or DF Malan Airport, where there was an open viewing deck. Sometimes we went with Ivan just to see the planes take off and to eat a snack in the cafeteria. That was a good outing, and the one to the harbour too, where we could go right on board to see the travellers' cabins. And what an occasion it was to see the boat being piloted out of the harbour with passengers on board unfurling colourful streamers in farewell!

The drives around the Peninsula were for admiring the beauty. There was no stopping and dipping a toe in the cold blue of the Atlantic Seaboard beaches because they were off-limits for skin colours like ours. It elicited no real hatred, though, being denied a place in the sun. That was the preserve of the teachers, the intellectual types and the *nouveau* middle class who had more to lose. And perhaps more time to spare to ponder what could and should have been if only *they* ruled the world, or at least the country.

We went to dams like Wemmershoek and Steenbras, collecting permits from the City Council offices at Newlands Swimming Pool. We climbed the Constantia Nek route at least twice a year and went as far as Healy Hutcheson and Woodhead dams on the eastern part of Table Mountain. And when visitors came, we went up by cable car and walked down via Nursery Ravine.

We travelled along all the eastern range mountain passes or up the N7 on a long journey to Goedverwacht Mission Station to visit with Great-grandpa Joe's friends even though he was long dead and buried. It was something my mom's family had been doing since 1928. It was the same when it came to visiting long-dead Great-grandma Sophie's siblings and their offspring who still lived near *Die Ou Pastorie* in Lourens Road, Somerset West.

Their homes were protected from the Group Areas removals by the Methodist Church, who defiantly said, 'This is our land, which we lease to our congregation. The houses are what they built, and they shall not be moved.'

Thus, whites moved in around them on Lourens Road, on land that did not belong to the church.

Always we had to pack eats and drinks so we wouldn't have to stop at segregated shops in small towns. Non-whites were not allowed to enter these shops and had to make purchases at a side entrance, usually a window counter.

Both Mavie's parents had been only children, so their cousins became my mom and her siblings' 'cousin uncles' and 'cousin aunts' all rolled into one. We visited them in Somerset West about eight times a year, including milestone birthdays and funerals – the latter held at the historic Methodist Church in Church Street, where great-grandma Sophie had been baptised in the 1870s. By the 1890s, she had moved to Rondebosch to work in service, but her family ties were so strong that her grandchildren still visited her family more than a hundred years later.

Such is the nature of the Cape: the removals may have broken families and communities, but the sense of knowing your place and who your family members were, remained strong. Sometimes we travelled by car to death-bed visits or funerals with Uncle Joey or Uncle Kenny, or the next-door neighbour, Mr Henry, in his old Pontiac. The maintenance of ties with extended family living in the 'country' was regarded as provincialism by outsiders and was mocked for being backwards.

The same strong ties went for great-grandma Minnie's family, whom we visited in Crawford and Claremont. Cousin Esmé's home stood on the land where Cavendish Square was later built. When the removals started, they made a wise choice to move to newly built Elfindale. The suburb was bordered by Heathfield, Diep River and Southfield, and was a mere ten-minute walk from Meadowridge close to the natural beauty of the Little Princessvlei.

Ordinary Sunday afternoon visits to Somerset West required a long train journey. The morning began at 11 am with a walk to Lansdowne Station, followed by a change at the scary Salt River Junction for the Strand train. The industrial areas were deserted on Sundays and the eerie-looking factories and the grime of the railway junctions at Salt River or Maitland made it all seem un-friendly. And then there was the rush across the metal bridges spanning multiple tracks, which just seemed to me like a recipe for disaster.

It was always just Dor, Stella, Mavie and me on these journeys. It just looked plain dangerous out the window, especially Ndabeni and Maitland. The adults kept me awake pointing out sights, but I must have tuned out. I only remember the names Firgrove and Faure and fields full of cows. At last, we were in Somerset West, on the walk to Lourens Road with its *sloots* of clear running water which we crossed on a little concrete bridge. This brought us to the front garden of the Hurling family home. The matriarch, Aunty Callie, had been great-grandma Sophie's sister, and her children – who were Mavie's second cousins Milly, Dan, Doy and Clairy – still lived there. Her other son and his family lived opposite, near the Catholic church.

The garden had a giant oak with a radius of about one metre, and around its base was a flowerbed filled with pansies. It looked like a fairy circle straight out of a children's storybook. There were also hyacinths, roses, hydrangeas, foxgloves and sweet peas trailing up cane sticks.

On the wide red polished *stoep* were chairs and pot plants. The Hurling family also had a side and a back *stoep*. Their garden wasn't as big as ours in Lansdowne, but it was as charming, with a huge mulberry tree seeming to grow out of the side of the garage. The house felt like home too, thanks to the wood-burning stove.

The Hurlings spoke English to us, rather than allow us to mangle their beloved Afrikaans, even though Stella prided herself on being fluent in Afrikaans. Dor couldn't be bothered about language; she spoke the language of flowers and gardens. Mavie and the aunties never visited empty-handed, and teatime was quite an occasion with cakes, savouries and the ubiquitous *soetkoekies* that tasted of spices, with just a hint of ginger.

The Somerset West family was the realm of *suikerbrood* that was baked in a 20-cm deep ring cake tin. It wasn't like the traditional Dutch *suikerbrood*. It was lighter in texture, more like a sponge cake thanks to the twelve eggs in the mixture, this according to Cousin Clarice, the *suikerbrood* Queen. Much later she dictated the recipe to Cousin Lee-Lee, a tall, lanky teen who came armed with notebook and pen to write down recipes in preparation for future husband, children, home and hearth.

Once or twice the family took us for a hike around the Helderberg Nature Reserve. The visits always felt too short. Then it was back to the long train journey home, with freshly baked bread from the Portuguese bakery on Main Road tucked into Stella's cloth-covered wicker basket. By the time we arrived in Salt River, it would be getting dark, and by Lansdowne, it was fully dark.

When we went by car, we had to pack in as many visits as possible to the other family members who lived elsewhere in Somerset West. If we didn't visit them, we'd be reminded of this oversight the next time we saw them.

The Gordons and Vissers, great-grandma Sophie's nephews and nieces, lived in areas closer to the wine farms. When these areas were declared white, they bought homes in the housing scheme Servitas, near the huge De Beers plant for armaments on the N2. Visits to Servitas were only possible when we went by car.

The area had a rich red clay soil and cousin Ernie Gordon was king of the dahlias and roses, while the garden of his brother Leonard looked like Namaqualand with rocks, *vygies,* towering cacti, and a few thorny rose bushes. Grapevines bearing the sweetest grapes grew on pergolas in both their backyards.

They all feared a second round of removals to Faure or Macassar. These fears were spoken of in hushed tones and gestures heavy with uncertainty.

As a child, I realised there were scandals in the country towns just as there were in the city, whispered secrets of the hidden lives of others, carefully worded confidences of hurt and betrayal, rage and tears, shame and scorn.

It is not my place to tell those tales. Instead, I will throw my lot in with my dearly departed family who chased points of light wherever they found them, all the days of their lives – as if the lights were the rarest and most elusive butterflies floating on the breeze.

A few times a year we would go to Goedverwacht, a secluded Moravian mission station in the Piketberg Mountains. This tradition of visiting Mr Julius's family started in 1928. Great-grandpa Joe had the cartage contract on a De Hoop building site, where he met and befriended Mr Julius who worked on the building crew.

The Goedverwacht visits were planned months in advance. We had to get up at 4.30 am on a Sunday to go on a trek up the N7 in a convoy of two or three cars. This was in case there was a breakdown – the other drivers were there to help fix.

This arrangement was an absolute necessity in a family of crock-car owners. Uncle Kenny with his mechanical know-how was the favoured asset to take on the journey, but he and his family didn't always go along. Sometimes it was the neighbours, the Henry family in their Pontiac, or Uncle Joey and family, or any of the other friends. Once or twice, Granny Davids, Aunty Doreen and Uncle Julian went with us, when Ivan was working and couldn't make it.

In my early teens, fuel tanks had to be filled before 1 pm on a Saturday, before the petrol stations closed, only to reopen on Monday morning. During the oil crisis of 1973, Arab countries placed an embargo on the supply of oil to Western countries, including

South Africa, in retaliation for their support of Israel. This resulted in petrol rationing and restricted trading hours.

Jerry cans of water were loaded in the boot before all else. We had to be on the road by 5.30 am at the latest, before the sun was scorching, or else the car radiators were likely to overheat by the time we got to De Hoop. And De Hoop wasn't the end destination: we still had to tackle the mountain pass west after that.

Food was packed, of course, with breakfast on the road at a picnic spot halfway between the Philadelphia and Malmesbury turnoffs. My earliest memory of the road north was of endless hills with endless farms with lone trees on the horizon, cows, and fields of sunflowers, wheat and lupin for cattle feed. It was a prettier drive than along the N7 in its current form, but a lot slower too.

I always felt relief when I spotted the lone tree on the hill at Moorreesburg because it signalled that we were nearing the end of the journey. Then the silos at De Hoop, which heralded the Velddrif turn off. Sometimes we'd be on the pass in time to see the steam train below in the valley through which the Berg River flowed. The train would be chugging into Moravia Station on its journey to Namaqualand, and then on to South West Africa, long before it became Namibia.

We passed Wittewater, lying isolated in the distance, just before we reached the gravel road to Goedverwacht. It was a long way in, past farms, vineyards and vegetable patches. Then we rounded the bend into the valley with its one road and saw the single row of houses perched on the mountainside, going all the way round in a horseshoe shape.

Down the centre of the horseshoe grew lush gardens tended by the villagers, each for their own household. Access to the gardens was over thick wooden planks embedded in the grassy embankments between which water diverted from the river ran in a *sloot* adjacent to the gravel main road. This *leiwater* was used to irrigate the gardens.

The thatched-roof white-washed houses had uncovered *stoeps*, so you couldn't sit in the shade like at home or in Somerset West. Some modern conversions sported sandstone finishes, twentieth-century roofing and indoor plumbing. The houses were built close to the road, while the backyards stretched about a quarter way up the mountain. They usually contained a kitchen garden with the ubiquitous grapevine, a stinky pigpen, a hen house and an outhouse. It could have been anywhere in continental Europe.

There was a primary school, established in 1846 – where Mr Julius's daughter *Juffrou* Settie taught – an old mill, a shop which was closed on Sundays, a post office and the Moravian Church. The whole place was steeped in mission history. Nowadays, Goedverwacht is part of the Mission Station Route tours. When my family used to visit, we were usually the only outsiders there on any given Sunday and we were the entertainment for the day.

The gardens were wonderful: oranges and lemons still on the trees in spring, massive pumpkins, potatoes, squash, carrots, onions, beetroot, cauliflower, cabbages, bananas, paw-paws, guavas – and custard apples, of all fruits. The latter never failed to fascinate my avid gardening family, and Stella managed to grow one in a pot. She transplanted the tree into her own garden a few years later and it bore fruit once or twice.

Gardens seemed to connect people back then: growing food, providing sustenance to families, swopping cuttings, seeds and tips. Depending on the season, we'd walk to the river to pick *kruisement* and *buchu,* which Dor liked to drink as a herbal tea.

Once we climbed the mountain with one of Mr Julius's teacher sons, Meneer Hennie, to see a cave with cave art. In later years, as the city crept in to contaminate the village, graffiti was found on the cave walls.

Mr Julius's children had moved to Cape Town and become teachers. The youngest daughter, Phinie, took up nursing at Somerset Hospital and later became a matron at Tygerberg Hospital. We went to their weddings in Goedverwacht. We also attended the funerals at the church, with women sitting on one side and men on the other side of a wooden partition, as per the Moravian tradition.

The church band used to blow up an off-key storm. For burials the band would lead the way, playing funeral dirges, and the people would be singing their slow hymns in keening, mournful tones. On we would walk to the cemetery across the valley, through somebody's garden, and always it would be boiling hot.

In memory, it was like being in a movie. As an adult, I would see movies at Cinema Nouveau set in Provence, Holland, Spain, Italy, Greece, Mexico, Australia, Argentina, Chile, Japan and the American Deep South. The scenes would be slow, dusty and timeless, unknowable depths beneath the surface, and they would always remind me of Goedverwacht.

In my teen years, I decided that one day I would live in such a village somewhere on the West Coast to write books, isolated, quiet, in step with nature and its seasons. I was disabused of this idea with: 'You can't live here, you are not Moravian and your family has no blood ties to the land.'

Oh well, another pipe dream nuked.

In the afternoon, after tea and cake, we said our goodbyes and left for the city, the boot filled with country produce and goodwill. We usually headed back the same way, but when the coast road was upgraded, we'd drive further west to Velddrif where the *bokkoms* (salted fish) could be seen drying out on lines strung between blue gum trees.

It was always dark by the time we got back from Goedverwacht. Those vast, empty country spaces were a far cry from the city in the south, systematically being pulverised, its soul rotting while its inhabitants shrilly boasted about how beautiful it was.

No matter how far my family ventured out and how often, home with its own set of problems would still be there, waiting for the right moment to strike, leaving us all gasping for breath.

Excision

EVERYTHING WAS IN flux. There was constant change.

What were the apartheid rulers worried about: that people would grow to be better? The possibility that there was enough space and were enough resources for all to improve by reasonable means was not even considered.

The Group Areas Act was a cornerstone of apartheid's system of racial segregation and economic and political discrimination. It was passed into law in 1950 and had several incarnations. The Act effectively restricted non-whites to certain designated areas where they could live and own businesses. These areas weren't pretty although, no matter where you go in Cape Town, there are surprisingly beautiful views of Table Mountain. And the further away from the Table Mountain range, the closer you are to the Eastern ranges and these are spectacular in the first light of dawn. However, they were always far from the economic hub and out-of-sight-out-of-mind for whites. And it swung both ways: whites were unlikely to show up and put a damper on the life on the Cape Flats.

People of colour who stayed in largely mixed suburbs in Cape Town, and above the suburban and Cape Flats railway lines, were forced to leave those areas. Many of them owned property, their families having resided for hundreds of years in the suburbs along the mountainside, all the way from Sea Point to Simon's Town, Kirstenbosch and Constantia, and all along the northern routes such as Voortrekker and Ysterplaat roads.

One by one, families were moved out, their living restricted to smaller pockets of land in suburbs further away from the city. The commute to work often entailed journeys of up to two hours, with interchanges along the way.

The forced removals began in the 1950s and lasted well into the 1980s. Thirty years of upheaval.

For me, apartheid was about where not to sit. Outside benches, seats in the bus, carriages on the train, beaches, campsites, restaurants, certain parts of hospitals and medical surgeries. Sitting down was complicated.

And there were separate toilets everywhere: City Council public toilets and toilets on the stations and business premises. Even the black maid who raised her madam's children had her own toilet outside. She wasn't allowed to be with her young white charges in the park but had to stand at the entrance while a park attendant took them to play on the swings.

To the imaginative girl that I was, apartheid seemed to be largely about toilets and benches. And bulldozers and concrete. Some industries – like sanitary ware and plumbing suppliers, architects, engineers, the entire construction industry, in fact – must be making poo-loads of money, I thought. It must have been profitable building and cementing racial segregation.

But mostly apartheid was just plain contradictory.

If you made the effort to travel to Table Mountain, starting at Kirstenbosch, or if you were to climb the mountain via any of the tracks like Skeleton Gorge, Nursery Ravine or Constantia Nek to the top, there was no segregation. Nor was there any at the Cape

Point nature reserve, climbing to the top of the lookout at the lighthouse or even riding up in the little bus. Or travelling to the top of Table Mountain in the cable car, or going to Wynberg Park or Kirstenbosch Gardens or Maynardville Park or Claremont Gardens or the Company Gardens in the city centre, hiking along the Pipe Track or the Contour Path all the way around the mountain. Or if you went to Ou Kaapseweg or Silvermine Nature Reserve, went camping at Duiker's Klip or Signal Hill or Chapman's Peak where there were picnic and braai spots. In all these places it was as if apartheid did not exist.

On footpaths out in nature, greetings were cordial across the colour lines, and everyone simply went their way or minded their own business. Apartheid could not segregate the majesty of Cape nature and the mountain. Even the telescope on Table Mountain could be used by everyone. All you needed was the right coins.

By the 1970s, when my teens started, the forced removals were in full swing. Some of our neighbours had moved in the 1950s from Newlands and Cape Town to our road, thinking that Lansdowne would not be affected by the segregation laws. And they had also surmised that the whites would not want to live so far down the mountain.

There were stories of non-white property owners in places such as Kloof Nek who saw the writing on the wall and sold before being forced to sell and they received market value. One such owner was able to buy a farm in Diep River, land that eventually became the upmarket coloured garden village suburbs Elfindale, Windsor Park and Punt's Estate. Many owners who sold their properties in places like Claremont, Newlands, Mowbray and the city centre were able to buy huge houses in Wynberg, the only coloured area above the Cape Flats railway line that the apartheid rulers weren't able to destroy.

By the time owners were forced to sell, they received about a quarter of the market value of their property. One owner, who sold in District Six in the 1950s, bought a massive two-plot property in Claremont, but his children were forced to sell at less than market value after his death in the mid-1960s.

Many people in the mixed neighbourhoods – because they were mixed – had created good lives for themselves by the 1960s, with stories to share. But as District Six fell, Newlands, Claremont and other areas in the south started to feel the rumblings.

A huge shadow was cast by the men from 'The Group', as the community referred to the people who enforced the Group Areas Act. They came knocking at all hours, suitably attired in the pinnacle of Nationalist sartorial elegance: short safari suits and long socks. Officiously holding clipboards, they would ask the same questions over and over again. 'Who owns this property? Where is the owner? How many people live here?'

Parents who were looking forward to a life of steady growth, hoping to see their hard work pay off and their children educated and growing into better lives and times, found themselves having to scramble around for back-up plans. Once these officials were at your door delivering the 'your numbers up' letter, it was a struggle to find a new home to take your family to.

People were sad and weary as they trudged from the City Council to the Divisional Council Housing Offices to put their names on lists. Worse yet was the humiliation of being told they earned too little to own their own home and had to settle for a tiny flat in one of those impersonal blocks that sprung up all over the Cape Flats. (The latter name does not derive from the blocks of flats, though, but from the low-lying areas outside the city limits.)

Every day neighbours would drop by our house to tell their

stories. They talked mostly to Mavie and Ivan, who always made time for a word or two with whoever put their feet over the threshold. I was an introverted and not very sociable child and the two of them were hard acts to follow. So I didn't follow. Maybe just a little, later on in life, but half-heartedly.

One such neighbour who walked up the yard when she saw Mavie outside was Miss Dorothy Fisher who, in 1969, was the first woman and the fifth recipient overall of a Professor Christiaan Barnard heart transplant and, at more than twelve years with her new heart, the longest survivor of his first batch of operations. She came to talk to Mavie before the op because that's what people did: they came to speak to the McBains. And what they confided, never came back to them via some other route. My aunties, uncles and parents were the height of discretion. Well, all those stories had to have gone somewhere – they stuck like glue in this old memory of mine.

After the operation, when Miss Dorothy could walk again, she came to show Mavie her scar. This was after the hoo-ha had died down and she was no longer a medical celebrity. People had stopped driving by to ogle the Fishers' humble home and delivery vehicles had ceased lining up on the road to deliver gifts to her door. The stories of Miss Dorothy being wooed by the uncles in the furniture and retail business spread far and wide. Even the whites from as far as Crawford came to see the home of the most famous woman in our area.

That scar was a shock to my seven-year-old self. It stretched from her throat to below her navel. It was quite a wide cut, at least seven centimetres or more, and ochre yellow in colour, a few shades darker than Miss Dorothy's skin tone. Mavie insisted that I had to see and listen to the patient's tale of having been cut right through the bone.

I heard about the heart being removed, the split-second exchange of hearts, and how long she was out for the count. There was no such thing as 'sensitive viewer, kindly turn away from this sight' in Mavie's book. Reality had to be known or else it would trap you later on in life. Besides, it was history, right there before our eyes, and when would I get to see that again?

Grandpa Jack had hopes that I would grow into a medical frame of mind. I tried, studying nursing in my early 20s, but those youthful visions of scars and sores and pain and death were a strong deterrent.

By 1971, when the delete button was being pressed on one neighbour after the other, the Fisher family were removed from Dale Street on a government truck to a Lotus River flat on Fifth Avenue. Miss Dorothy lived a long time in spite of the operation and the move. Ivan used to see her regularly when he worked out that way, during his incarnation as a traffic cop.

Of all my chommies Celie was the first to leave. She moved to Bellville South with her mom, to stay with her uncle, Cousin Norman, another of Grandpa Jack's cousins, who was a teacher at Alexander Sinton High School. Next went Uncle Joey and family to the other side of the Cape Flats railway line, to an owner-build home in Pinati Estate which bordered on Hanover Park. With him went his children and grandchildren who I used to play with.

The next-door neighbours and other regular visitors at our house moved to Hanover Park, and still others to Lotus River and Grassy Park. Many of the old people died before they had to move. Ivan and Mavie went to a lot of funerals.

One heart-broken old man from down Dale Street, the father of a family friend, hanged himself in his garage. I went with Mavie to see what was happening with the cop vans and ambulance rushing by and the neighbours standing outside. We got there in time to see the body being cut from the rafters.

I thought about his daughter. We'd just gone to see her off to England on the ship. We stood there, Mavie and me and all the neighbours, until the police vans and the ambulance had all gone.

By age ten most of my old chommies were gone, and the rest had found other interests. I turned to books, *Nancy Drew* and the *Hardy Boys* series, and to the science magazine *Look and Learn*. Sometimes I sneaked a look at Meneer Wilfie's closely guarded *Life Magazines* or his *National Geographics*. My craft work kept me busy too, and I always had pop tunes on the radio for company.

In Claremont, Granny Davids and Aunty Doreen in Chichester Road, and Meneer Wilfie and his family in Escher Street, were getting more frequent visits from the removals officials.

Stella had Claremont friends who'd moved to Australia, while others had gone to Canada. She often dragged me along for company when she went to say her farewells. To this day I remember where the houses were and how they looked inside, but not the people's names. Other friends of Stella moved to Grassy Park, and their piano had to stand in our passage for a while. Her more uppity friends moved to Fairways, instead of Australia which was where they really wanted to be. I'd prayed fervently that God would grant them their wish, but those prayers came to nought.

I went to many of the suburbs affected by forced removals. Going to central Cape Town was never a big factor in my existence, however. It was a chore Mavie did once a month to pay the electricity, water and rates accounts. Before I went to school, and later on when it was school holidays, I'd go with her, travelling by train from Lansdowne or by bus from Claremont.

Always the same routine: pay the accounts, have a look at some clothing stores, then up Castle Street so Mavie could gaze with longing at the beautiful crockery at Foster's. One time, she intended to buy a coat but spotted a white porcelain tea set adorned with delicate violets for R4.95, so she bought that instead. A good English tea set was far more important to her than owning a fake brown fur coat to wear to the opera.

From there we'd cut across to Church Street to pay Ivan's monthly fee for the SA Association of Artists. We would spend some time admiring the paintings, then cross over to the Argus building to look at the photos in the outside display windows.

Sometimes we went to the Company Gardens to feed the squirrels and walk around the pond and the aviary. Then back down to Darling Street and to Wellington Fruit Growers to buy fruit mix and other cake ingredients.

The Grand Parade with all the merchandise stalls held no real fascination for Mavie, and we seldom went that way if month-end happened to fall on a Wednesday. Sometimes we'd go look at material to have dresses or coats made by Aunty Edna, who'd have preferred to make only elaborate beaded wedding dresses for thin young women.

We also had to go to the Central Post Office to buy stamps for the surgery where Dor worked. The interior was a grand hall, beautiful and stately. It's hard to believe that the entire post office system has fallen into such chaos from what it once was. At month's end, I helped Dor fold the patients' accounts into envelopes and *plak* stamps on the front.

In the city, we'd eat lunch at an eatery called La Fiesta. Nothing fancy, just beef sandwiches with lettuce and tomato and tea.

It was upstairs in one of the buildings on Darling Street and was the only place non-whites could eat in the city centre in those years. If memory serves me correctly, the owners were forced to close because non-whites weren't allowed to run businesses in white areas.

In later years, the OK Bazaars on Adderley Street had a place we would eat lunch, pies mostly, and way before apartheid ended Garlicks on Adderley Street also opened up their restaurant to all customers.

For the return trip from the city by train we had to use the upstairs concourse because the main concourse was for whites only. The Golden Acre and the bus terminus hadn't been built yet and if we were travelling by bus, we'd wait outside the flower sellers at Victoria Place on Adderley Street, to catch the Retreat or Wynberg bus. The snapdragons and the freesias, with their distinctive fragrance, always caught my attention.

At times when I had to go to Somerset Hospital to see some medical specialist, we'd wait in the same place for the Green Point bus. Mavie, of course, loved going to Somerset to *kekkel* with her friends, who were all nursing sisters and matrons by then.

On those trips to the city we didn't take much note of the 'white' world around us, because we were focused on the list of places we needed to go to.

I never visited District Six while it still stood. We didn't know anyone who lived there. We saw the bulldozing from the bus, though. Mavie just pointed it out to me but did not elaborate. One month there'd be buildings and the next month there was nothing. It was like viewing a serialised movie titled *Total Demolition*. All that was left after a few years was a gravel scar on the mountainside and, poignantly, the St Marks Church, standing alone in a suburb that had been razed. All eyes on the bus turned to the stone building where God dwelt[6].

Meneer Wilfie, whose school Roggebaai in Green Point was moved and became Vista High in the Bo Kaap, always carried his Pentax camera with him. Every afternoon, before leaving the city, he'd walk to District Six to photograph the demolition, in black and white or in colour slides. Some of his friends taught at schools close to the destruction, and they told stories of their pupils being in class one day and the next day they were gone.

Back in Claremont Mavie and I either took the short cut through OK Bazaars to the terminus for the buses heading east, or we'd go past the Claremont flower sellers.

There was a definite rhythm to the days of my childhood that had to be rearranged when the removals upended everything.

In my early years, I had no point of reference when it came to understanding adult emotions, but the sadness and anxiety were always a steady hum. It sometimes erupted in anger over something small that could have been sorted out calmly, had it not been for the constant stress of living under apartheid.

---

6 It is one of history's ironies that the apartheid authorities did not touch holy land. The sandstone churches belonging to the Anglican Church that dot the slopes of Table Mountain remained the places of worship for congregants who'd been forcibly removed from their homes. They came from as far away as Eersterust and Bonteheuwel to worship at St Mark's in District Six, Good Shepherd Church in Kirstenbosch, All Saints and St Aidan's in Lansdowne, St Andrews in Newlands, St Saviour's, St Mathews and Christ the King in Claremont, St Paul's in Rondebosch and St John's in Wynberg. So too, Muslims continued to attend mosque or visit holy shrines in areas they used to live.

As 'natural enemies' of the Calvinist Protestant state, the Catholic churches were a law unto themselves. With the advent of apartheid they remained multi-racial as they'd always been. Priests officiated at multi-racial weddings, which in terms of The Prohibition of Mixed Marriages Act were illegal and could result in jail time for the non-white partner in the marriage.

There weren't too many arguments in my presence. Ivan and Mavie quarrelled behind closed doors. But I do remember the tension that seemed to emanate from all the adults. I became adept at reading expressions, moods and body language.

It was so exhausting, always anticipating the next flare-up.

I didn't have words back then for what I perceived around me. I lived on my nerves, on high alert, constantly afraid of unforeseen outbursts. There were neighbours who would come in and *skel* about a dog running into their place, or that they didn't like the hedge growing so wild. Or Uncle Joey and Mavie would have a set-to. And the eruptions didn't only happen at home. You could go to Niefies and get shouted at just for being a little kid, even if you weren't the little kid an adult actually wanted to shout at. People were always venting unexpectedly. Negotiating the world of adults was like stepping into an emotional minefield.

Life felt monochromatic, a silent movie that rolled on and on, with those jumps in the celluloid that appeared as lines on the screen. The movie never stopped or burned out, the projector never broke down. It just kept reeling on, even as characters departed one by one, and we knew the film would soon have to jump out of its sprockets.

Or maybe it was like the movie *Schindler's List*, shot in black and white except for the red coat worn by a little girl. The colour in the adults' monochromatic movie appeared intermittently when suppressed emotions erupted in rage – or silly-jokes laughter which sounded like that particular kind of fake that signalled that carefully made masks were about to crack.

Focusing on staying sane and holding everything together meant that the adults didn't have to think, they just had to do. They had to keep on keeping on. The movie had to roll on.

Up, down Lansdowne Road

THERE WAS SO much going on around us in the area we'd soon be erased from, all we could do was look, listen and let it happen. Church and school held their dwindling communities together as best they could.

Bulldozers started in on the houses on Dale Street directly opposite us. We hurried by and said nothing. At least two Dale Street families ended up living in army tents on the field at the end of Trevor Road. The Divisional Council organised homes for them in the newly built Lotus River flats and eventually, the government trucks came to move them off the field.

The family who lived directly opposite the Norfolk pine tree went to Australia. Others in our street decided England was a better option. Sometimes one family member left the country while the rest moved to Steenberg, to Lavender Hill, to rent wherever they could, never really finding a home again.

At least two sets of neighbours came to stay with us before taking the boat to England. And always, the old men singing 'Auld Lang Syne'.

'You gloss over feelings and what people suffered', an early reader told me about this narrative. It's an old stoicism. I learned it from the people I knew. There was much wiping away of tears, but pragmatism always won out and sadness was stuffed deep down inside.

There were no Oprah or Doctor Phil-type collective healing sessions. No trauma counselling, no crying room at the police stations. There were no health spas for respite. There were no freely available social welfare services – those only came later, to serve the uniform three-storey blocks of flats that were built facing one another that sprung up fast and furiously all over the Cape Flats.

You sank or you swam.

And you moved on, you did what you could. There was no available money or time for feelings – there was just too much to get done.

I had no friends left in my neighbourhood. I had acquaintances who had their own set of friends. Then they too moved away. At primary school, I chatted to other children, but those friendships didn't spill over to home. Sometimes over weekends, I had cousins and visitors' children for friends.

Could one really develop lasting ties when the times were not only changing but were ephemeral as well?

And you never knew what to expect. To be constantly vigilant and on guard was exhausting.

Feelings? What were they? I was not even eleven years old and, like most children across the Peninsula, I had seen and heard too much that was incomprehensible.

Life, I figured, was just plain *bladdie* ugly.

I built in checks and balances and learned to filter out what was good or bad, and who was good or bad. No matter how much Mavie, Ivan, the aunties and others would enthuse about something or someone being nice, I felt I could see what moved beneath the surface of things.

What did the young ones know back then? The prevailing

culture was that children should be seen and not heard. They played or went to school – they were certainly not consulted about anything. They did not meddle in adult business. They were not the centre of attention like it is today, and their egos were not indulged.

When it came time to move, they packed in their meagre possessions and their toys, if they had any, got on the truck with the rest of the family and moved. Often without fair warning, without saying goodbye.

Children sometimes came home from school to find their families had moved. Their furniture on the pavement, their house demolished. A kindly aunt or neighbour would be sitting outside, waiting to take care of them until the family returned to collect them and the rest of their furniture. Decades later I was to hear this same story told many times when photographer Tracey Adams and I interviewed several people who had been removed and who were still fighting for restitution.

There was so much shame. It made people retreat into themselves. Neighbours no longer went over, reluctant to seem like they were probing or meddling. If there was praying going on, it happened silently.

The people in our neighbourhood – coloured and white – were working class. The removals brought the class distinctions that weren't so noticeable before into sharp focus. Apartheid was not just colour and ethnic coding, but economic coding as well. It moved some forward, some sideways.

It moved the majority backwards.

I entered my last two years at St Ignatius Primary, relieved that the school had not been moved from Claremont yet. Two neighbouring primary schools, Clareinch and St Matthew's, had already merged to become Portia Primary School in 'coloured' Lansdowne, east of the railway line. Broad Road Primary School from Wynberg had become York Road Primary and was, illogically, right next to Portia Primary.

By the time I reached my final year at St Ignatius, my plaits had grown so long and were so heavy that they caused headaches. My hair was cut short.

By now I was developing my own ideas, seeing that all else had failed around me. I read the British teen magazine *Jackie*, which I bought at Niefies Cafe for a few cents a month, all saved from my R1 pocket money a week. I paid the grand sum of R5 for my first LP at Garlick's in Cape Town – David Cassidy's *Cherish* – and listened to it on Stella's Pilot radiogram, which she'd bought from friends leaving for Australia.

Soon I had a growing collection of seven singles, including Deep Purple's 'Smoke on the water', The Temptations' 'Rolling down the mountainside', The Osmonds' 'And they call it puppy love', Michael Jackson's 'Ben' and a few others. I listened to Springbok Radio Hit Parade every afternoon at 5 pm.

They called to me, those tunes from far away. I wanted to know how it was that the singers sounded so happy and free, even though most of the lyrics were about heartbreak. By the end of primary school, I'd graduated to Golden Earring's *Radar Love* LP.

By October 1973 I'd been received into all three sacraments of initiation of the Catholic Church. All of these were celebrated at Our Lady Help of Christians in Lansdowne. I'd been baptised in 1961 when the church was only a few weeks old. I learnt to confess and then received Holy Communion in October 1968, with my Confirmation in 1973.

Remembrance of first holy Communion

Dor's first holy Communion certificate, 1939.

This sacrament, said the teacher, Mrs West, enabled the faithful to be sealed with 'the gift of the Holy Spirit'. The great big fear of the ceremony was when the bishop 'slapped' the candidate on the right cheek. There was talk of people fainting in shock in previous years. Would the slap hurt?

But the highly hyped smack turned out to be just a light tap on the cheek and a whispered 'Go in peace' from the bishop. The tap was a reminder for the confirmed to keep or defend the faith.

And that was that for primary school and me.

Things began to recede. Church, which had always been so central, going on all those visits, the scenic drives, the shows, the opera, all the people, being part of the extended family. When connections fade to grey, what remains are memories and snippets of music, the 'soundtrack of our lives'.

In my mind the music that fits that bridging time between primary and high school would have to be Mozart's 'Der Hölle Rache', commonly known as the Queen of the Night aria, from *Die Zauberflöte* and 'The Flower Duet' from the Leo Delibes opera *Lakmé*. Perhaps they were mental associations of being cast adrift or the severance from Mother Church and from my little patch of the motherland. Perhaps those soprano voices were a plaintive foreboding of the descent into obliteration in the Protestant fatherland of apartheid South Africa?

Perhaps acceptance had set in for Ivan, Mavie and the aunties. We were still touring the city, but less intensely. Over time, Ivan added driving through new areas, looking at houses on his touring route.

We went everywhere to see what was available: Belhar, Glenhaven, Elsies River, Ravensmead, Cravenby, Tiervlei, Uitsig, Bellville South, Grassy Park, Lotus River, Ocean View, Groenvlei, Welcome Estate, Vanguard Estate, Bellville South, Manenberg, Greenhaven, Hanover Park, Pinati Estate. And on the other side of the railway line: Lansdowne, Crawford, Kromboom, Belgravia, Bridgetown, Wynberg, Fairways, Punts Estate, Elfindale and Retreat.

We didn't know people in all those areas, but when we did, Ivan stopped for a visit. I found these visits exhausting. The more 'friends' Ivan made, the more weddings we went to. It was a case of knowing but not really knowing many people. It took so much time that could have been used elsewhere.

I could never make out what Ivan hoped to achieve by attempting to be 'all things to all people'. Why couldn't he just stay at home and paint pictures or read a book, I thought, instead of running around in circles like a headless chicken?

Incidentally, Ivan always had books he carried around with him, but he never actually read them. He never sat in a chair to read a book from cover to cover. If he had it would surely have given him the wisdom he needed to choose a path for the future. Instead, he chose the mindlessness of small talk with shallow friends.

Maybe it was his curiosity about houses and interior design that drove Ivan to go in search of acquaintances who'd moved. Their new homes were mostly lovely and more modern than the old ones. We saw houses, townhouses, duplexes, scheme houses and council-built flats and cottages.

Above the heads of those who'd not yet found the place where they wanted to be, a bleakness hovered: on getting to know new people, having to travel further to work, with more than one bus or train. Uncertainty everywhere.

My favourite of the new houses was the one built by Mr Trevor, the architect who had lived down Dale Street. He'd moved to Fairways and Ivan found him there in 4th Avenue when we visited Grandpa Jack's cousins, the Hurlings, who lived in 5th Avenue. The rooms led off a covered courtyard with a pool or a pond in the centre of the space, which also had an exotic plant garden. A few years later Mr Trevor emigrated to Canada.

In Punt's Estate, Diep River, Cousin Norman's house was Spanish style, with a sunken lounge and a huge book-lined study and a beautiful courtyard that served as an outside entertainment area. The courtyard had roses, grapevines, a loquat tree and seating extending out of the side of built-in flower boxes. The house was unusual. This was where my old chommie Celie now lived. She was back in the southern suburbs after nearly seven years

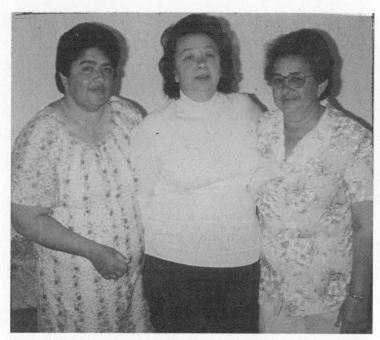

Mavie, Aunty Rosie from Joburg and Stella, 1980s.

in Bellville South, in time for high school at South Peninsula High. We talked about school, new school friends and books and all kinds of everything.

Meneer Hennie, the teacher who grew up in Goedverwacht, and his wife Mrs Mary had moved from their rented cottage in Kromboom to Grassy Park, where they constructed a garden that was a work of art. It sported roses, cacti and a rockery fishpond he built himself. Their back garden had fruit trees, a vegetable patch and an aviary with all kinds of parrots, budgies and canaries. Meneer Hennie made artworks too that spoke of the land, strong earthy works of pottery, no doubt inspired by his West Coast roots, and he created abstract paintings.

Mrs Janap, Mavie's operatic fairy godmother, who'd lived at 5 Heatherley, had moved to a lovely house her husband and sons built in the coloured part of Crawford. Mr Salie's children also favoured courtyards at the houses they built in Surrey Estate and Wetton.

Of course we, the children, were afraid and insecure about the future. Who wouldn't be? But we kept things bottled up inside. Later, the pain manifested in different ways. Some of my peers left school early, or had babies in their teens, or went to sea to work on the boats. No one is unaffected by being uprooted. They weren't called 'forced removals' for nothing.

Yet, there was no protest action, no community meetings. There probably were underground political meetings, but most people didn't know about them. We heard of people being arrested or fleeing the country or being sent to Robben Island, but this was not general knowledge. The apartheid government rammed any resistance into the earth from which it arose. Information hard to come by and the full story, in print or on film, was suppressed.

I'd heard of our opposite neighbour Eric Petersen fleeing to Germany. I knew about Dennis Brutus, who had campaigned to get South Africa banned from the 1964 Tokyo Olympics, having to leave for England on an exit permit. There was a story doing the rounds that Dennis Brutus had escaped off Robben Island by swimming out to sea and had been picked up by a boat en route to England.

I'd heard that Neville Alexander, my cousin Joline's Livingstone High class teacher, was sitting on Robben Island. We all knew about Imam Abdullah Haron, who'd died in police detention at the hands of the Security Branch in 1969. He was a Muslim cleric, an anti-apartheid activist and editor of *Muslim Views*.

I heard these things as I drew or made crafts near the grownups, eavesdropping on the grownups' conversation in the kitchen. I'd always known about the arrests. Ivan's eldest brother Uncle

Cyril had been arrested. He was detained for a few weeks and had been beaten so severely he had scars on his back for the rest of his life. The cops had come to raid Granny Davids' house. After that family members were paranoid about being followed and having their phones tapped.

That was not unusual – many people believed the authorities tapped their phones and that they were being followed by security police. Also, that their neighbours were on the payroll of the Security Branch and were spying on them. The prevailing paranoia meant that people thought the worst of each other. It was uncomfortable, unpleasant and unhealthy.

Those who travelled overseas on holiday, especially tour groups of teachers, believed that they were followed. I imagined the Security Branch to have a huge budget if they were able to send a cop on every tour undertaken by a group of coloured teachers. It must have been very entertaining and illuminating for them.

Ivan believed the phone at our house was tapped. He said when he left for work one morning at 6.30 am a Post Office technician was working on the line outside our house. (The separation of Post and Telecommunications only occurred in the 1980s.)

In later years, I checked with some old Telkom technicians and they confirmed the bugging of phones did indeed happen but said that the police installed their own equipment. These police technicians were based in a building situated near City Park Hospital. Post office phone technicians weren't allowed to fix phones on certain floors at police stations. There were things the police didn't want outsiders to see. Phone-tapping devices were sometimes found by telephone technicians in the units on the telephone poles. Technicians told me that at the telephone exchanges they would listen in on people's conversations, but for their own amusement, not for the police.

Uncle Cyril was prominent in Ivan's family, but I didn't really speak to him. I always felt uncomfortable in his company, because he used haughty tones while delivering cutting or sarcastic comments. After his arrest, he divorced himself from political resistance. He became a Freemason instead. Many artisans, carpenters, plumbers, electricians and printers were Freemasons – brothers in the international order that was established to help and offer fellowship to members. When it came to emigration, Masonic membership secured employment in host countries.

Uncle Cyril religiously attended the lodge in Newlands and participated in the secret ceremonies. When he died in the 1980s, his funeral service was held at St Mary Magdalene's in Lentegeur, though he wasn't Catholic. His burial was Masonic.

Ivan never attended church. He followed the teachings of the Rosicrucian Order and tirelessly quested for esoteric knowledge. He was not a member of the Order, but many old men in the community were. Ivan ordered their magazines by mail and dabbled in reading those, but just a bit here and there. He had a Holy Bible, a Quran, a Bhagavad Gita and a Dictionary of the Occult. To cover all bases, I suppose.

Meneer Wilfie's father, with whom he had a strained relationship, had belonged to the Rosicrucian Order. As the eldest son, he was tasked with burning all his father's books when he died. This was so that 'secret' knowledge would not fall into the hands of the uninitiated. Some two decades later, after Ivan had died, some old men came to visit me and asked me what I'd done with his books. Their approach was rather theatrical, voices lowered to confidential whispers and facial expressions arranged to convey some sort of grim warning that my answer had better be what they expected. It wasn't. I'd donated them to Cafda Bookshop. It would never have occurred to me to burn books. Oops.

About politics and journalism, Ivan would often mutter, but did not elaborate, 'Politics is a mug's game. Journalism is too.' Odd though that he had so many left-wing journalist friends. One of these later fled into exile and joined uMkhonto weSizwe.

As a child, I often heard about the Unity Movement, which was led by Aunty Doreen's friend Mr Richard Dudley, the science teacher and deputy principal at Livingstone High School. Mr Dudley had been at Livingstone since he started teaching in his early twenties, fresh out of the University of Cape Town. He served at the school for several decades but was always passed over for promotion to principal.

The same happened to many teachers who were deemed a threat to the government. They were denied promotion. Some were demoted. Cousin Norman was one of them. Some teachers were sent from city posts to country postings. There they served out time before returning to the city, but never back to their old schools and never to school leadership.

I didn't know much about the Unity Movement and always assumed it was for teachers and the intelligentsia. It seemed elitist, a club that the 'worthy' were invited to, to discuss an ideal political future for the country and to work on a ten-point plan. With tea in fine English porcelain cups and Tennis biscuits or Eet-Sum-Mors, homemade shortbread or buttered ginger loaf served on paper doily-covered plates.

All I knew was what the Movement stood for: equality for all people and rejection of the concept of race. And they believed in non-collaboration with any government institution. They were especially vocal about the Coloured People's Representative Council and later the Tricameral Parliament. The movement had a strategic plan and advocated boycott as a weapon of struggle. They also believed in the unity of all non-whites.

On the flipside of talk about the Unity Movement, Grandpa Jack's Cousin Cyril, also a Freemason, was brother-in-law to Mrs Alathea Jansen who had lived for decades in a double-storey house off Sir Alfred Avenue in our area. She was a member of the 60-member Coloured People's Representative Council. She too came up our yard to visit in the company of Cousin Cyril and his wife, Iris, her sister. In 1975, Mrs Jansen became the executive chairperson of the council which had limited legislative powers. In reality, the council was a token gesture to coloureds, to show that they had representation in the apartheid era and were not completely left out.

I remember Mrs Jansen telling the aunties and Mavie of her travels to Australia and New Zealand and the linking of women's groups engaged in housewifery and craft-making. It appeared that they were involved in creating stronger family structures so that there would be better communities. Role modelling seemed to be at the core of these structures.

She only came to visit a few times. I don't think she got what she was looking for from the aunties and Mavie. They were nice enough but were no leaders. Nice wasn't wanted. Push and drive and meddling demi-dictators were what was required to pull the whole sorry mess of people with more than 150 ancestral points of origin[7] into one representative voice. It was a tall order that

---

7   Research done by Patric Tariq Mellet found that coloureds or African Creoles were derived from 150 ancestral points of origin. More than 72 per cent come from Southern Africa, Sub-Saharan Africa and the islands off the West and East African coast. The second largest group came from all over the Indian Ocean, Mainland South East Asia (India, Ceylon, China, Taiwan, Vietnam, Malaysia and Pakistan), and Indian Ocean islands such as Java, Sumatra, Philippines, Timor and Selawesi. Other ancestral origins include Australian Aborigines, African Americans, Caribbeans, Japanese, Russians, Germans, Dutch, French and Portuguese.
Mellet, P.T. *Over 150 Tributaries in Coloured or Camissa (African Creole) Ancestry.* Camissa People: Cape Slavery and Indigene Heritage. https://camissapeople.wordpress.com/2019/04/18/chart-150-tributaries-in-coloured-or-camissa-african-creole-ancestry/ Last accessed 04/03/2020.

was never going to happen – and is unlikely to happen even today. The Nationalists tried spatial planning to make one shade of brown, but did it work? Politics was always a tricky track to follow, let alone understand.

The voice of non-white politics in Cape Town was always multidimensional, full of hard-to-follow nuance and meaning. The Nationalists tried cloning an entity that resembled their own political nature and voice with its flat-sounding theoretical rambling. They were lying more to themselves than to the people they tried to control. The non-white political domain was never just one or two choices. The threads of multiple origins were never buried but existed parallel to the surface and, on occasion, the past would intersect with the present and then just as suddenly fall back into the past again.

Unresolved hurts, centuries-old, lived on in following generations and manifested most notably in criminal behaviours such as the merchant gangs of the Cape Flat, but also in depression and anxiety and other mental health issues, and in chronic diseases.

In the desperate search for alternative homes in the 1970s, some people supported the Coloured Representative Council, in the mistaken belief that they would be rewarded with what they needed. It may have worked for some, but it didn't for others.

Much to Ivan's family's amusement, one of their sisters-in-law wrote to Prime Minister BJ Vorster for a house. They got one shortly afterwards in Belhar. What a move! In a way that was a big up-yours to the snobs in Ivan's family who prided themselves on having political sophistication. The inner circle of uncles, whom Cousin Thomas referred to as 'The Establishment' or 'The Plastic People', could not stop talking about that infamous letter at their little gatherings. Ivan made sure we went to visit the house that BJ Vorster himself had provided.

In 1973, Cousin Thomas, who lived with Granny Davids and Aunty Doreen, was in Standard 9 at Livingstone High. He and his friends formed an agit-prop performance group. Don't ask me what that stands for. I asked and I'm still waiting for an answer decades later – fancy-schmancy theatre folk. They wrote short skits which they performed at transport hubs to 'conscientise' people about the pitfalls of apartheid. They urged people to take a stand and to protest. No doubt, forced removals would have been number one on the agenda. A few times, the group was caught and ferried away to jail. Then Granny Davids would phone Ivan to come and take her and Aunty Doreen to get Thomas out. They were worried that he'd have an asthma attack. Returning after one such excursion to the police station, Ivan said he'd left his nephew there to sleep off his imbibing. Thomas dropped out of school that year, to pursue his passion for photography. It stood him in greater stead later on.

Everything I managed to gather about resistance to apartheid was from hearsay and not what I read. Most of the reading material that could possibly have provided a balanced view was banned, anyway. It was the worst possible situation, not knowing all sides to a story that would very much determine how well or badly one fared in the future that awaited you.

Trying to understand the extra-parliamentary climate of the 1970s was like going to a park where you swung on the swings, rode on the see-saw, climbed the jungle-gym or twirled around on the merry-go-round until you fell off dizzy. Battle lines were being drawn, but no one had a clue of who would fight where and how that fight would proceed and with what weapons, if any.

With a divided-down-the-colour-line family, I was party to stories from the other side too, through Uncle Willie from Lakeside and Aunty Rosie from Johannesburg. They had reclassified as white and left the fold in the mid-to-late 1950s, but they never abandoned Mavie and the other siblings.

Uncle Willie often visited when he was in the vicinity. He was softly spoken and often told us about his sons' escapades. The eldest one, Dudley, was fortunate enough to end up in the State President's Guard army unit that was based at the Cape of Good Hope Castle and not in a unit bound for the Angolan War. André, the youngest, had decided on a career in the SA Navy.

It was certainly a different kind of story from what we usually heard. Uncle Willie related to us who they dated, when and whom they married, and how many sons they had each. He told stories of middle-class success and other little domestic tales of home, hearth and family. He worked as a plumber at Old Mutual and was appalled by what he saw in the kitchens of the fanciest, most iconic hotels in the city. No, he said, he would never eat at The President Hotel, or The Heerengracht Hotel, or any of those places.

Uncle Willie's stories were not as dramatic as Auntie Rosie's. I don't think she had the capacity for banality. She could not shake a dyed-in-the-wool rebellious nature, no matter how much of a granny she was with her crafts. That woman's hands were busy all the time, knitting and crocheting and puffing away at her cigarettes, as she regaled her sisters with episode after episode of life in Joburg South.

They visited twice as a family when her daughters Linda and Marilyn were still in their teens, but out of school already. They drove down in their TJ-plated pale-blue Chevy straight out of a 'braaivleis, rugby, sunny skies and Chevrolet' advert.

The first time it was just Aunty Rosie, her husband, Uncle Gerry and their two daughters, and they stayed at Heatherley Road. The second time they came with their son James and his Afrikaner girlfriend Jeanette from Alberton and stayed with Uncle Willie in Lakeside. The girlfriend had yet to be briefed about why James was so gorgeously tanned and that it was not just from being one-eighth Portuguese.

Son and girlfriend hung out in Lakeside with the cousins while Aunty and the girls came to Lansdowne. James visited the aunties on his own when his girlfriend was distracted by some other planned activity. After that visit, Aunty Rosie flew down a few times with her very kind youngest daughter Marilyn, and also a few times on her own.

Aunty Rosie used the word *bliksem* a lot. One drama she told us, knitting needles clicking with pauses to puff on her Rothmans, was how James had been shot through the knee during the Angolan War. He went AWOL from the army from the military hospital in the Transvaal. The Military Police came looking for him at home, but she said she would *bliksem* them if they did anything to harm her son. She told them that to their faces, apparently. That woman was pure story gold.

Dor called her reclassified siblings 'recalcified'. For all her dry humour about the subject, she found herself 'recalcified' without even trying for white. She had filled in her forms 'coloured' for the green ID book circa 1981 (the one before the barcoded one), but the authorities looked at her picture, her name and surname, and calcified her.

Grandpa Jack had always been unimpressed by the 'recalcification' of two of his brood. He would mutter, 'When I lift my shirt, I'm white too.' And he was too, quite a pasty white. He thought their decision let the side down.

It wasn't a big deal for us. Many people had reclassified family. It was like having family that had emigrated – only the reclassifieds were still in the country. It didn't feel as though they were though. Emigrants and reclassifieds left their origins behind for the same reasons: opportunity, advancement and 'better lives for the children'. These people left for themselves and their nuclear family, not for anybody else.

Those who went overseas were also absorbed into white worlds. And those who went to visit them came back with stories of how it wasn't all that 'rosy' on the other side. I always thought they were lying.

The difference was that the reclassifieds made the most unpopular of choices available. But even though they did that, when they visited it was like when the overseas family came to visit. There was a short time of adjusting to each other's stories and then things continued as usual. And just like with the overseas family who visited us, they came to us because we couldn't go to them. Though Dor did visit Aunty Rosie. When Aunty Rosie came, it was like the past at the old house. She and the aunties would do crafts together and natter away, with Mavie contributing without needles and thread in hand. She'd be there, laughing at the stories. Mavie laughed a lot.

All were welcomed as the proverbial returning prodigals, whether from overseas or from the twilight zone of reclassification. There were great dangers close to home and many challenges that required extremely tiring focus rather than fretting over whether these family members visiting from white South Africa or overseas found one acceptable or not. Ultimately, everybody did their own thing and went their own way.

For Mavie and the aunties, the holes left in the family orbit by the reclassifieds were filled to some extent by extended family, neighbours and friends, but these could never fully replace those who lived far away. Rather it was like the words in Proverb 27.10, 'Never abandon a friend – either yours or your father's. When disaster strikes, you won't have to ask your brother for assistance. It's better to go to a neighbour than to a brother who lives far away.'

Of course, the old people and the aunties mourned the loss of seeing beloved grandchildren, nephews and nieces through their growing-up years. Their longing always spoke the loudest when photo albums were paged through and stories told of the faces on the pages who were either gone to other places or who had passed on.

Rebel

WHEN HIGH SCHOOL rolled around, I soon discovered that attending Livingstone High was a lot like taking a flying leap from St Peter's in the Vatican to the Kremlin in Moscow when Leon Trotsky was still in the politburo.

The year was 1974 and Cavendish Square had sprung up from the dust of the fallen homes of the removed. Kenilworth Centre on Racecourse Road and Werdmuller Centre on Main Road were under construction. And Checkers had two mini shopping centres in Claremont, one on Lansdowne Road near my new school and the other on Vineyard Road opposite Cavendish Square.

Roadworks began on the M5 and on the bridges crossing it at Lansdowne and Racecourse roads. The project took about two years to be completed. When Lansdowne Road was closed, traffic went via Racecourse and vice versa, until each bridge was completed. We had to walk to Racecourse Road for the bus.

High school was a bastion of opinion and irreverence, so different to the saintly atmosphere of primary school. I was surprised to see many of my old classmates at Livingstone. I imagined they would have gone on to the Catholic high schools – Immaculate High School for girls in Wynberg or St Columba's High School for boys in Athlone.

On the first day of school, we sat down to write an IQ test and, based on the results, we were academically streamed. I ended up in an academic class with the focus on science, maths and German. What I most wanted to study was art and geography, but Ivan and the teachers said no, not a chance, I had to take 'more academic' subjects.

At first, German was a novelty and I got an A for it at the end of Standard 6. But every year that followed I asked to shift to art class and every year I was turned down. I believe I would have enjoyed high school had I been allowed to study what I was good at.

I made friends among all the clever girls and boys. There were Carlyn, Michelle, Bonnie, Fatima, Dilshad, Celeste, Sandy, Latiefa, Joseph and many more. Things felt more light-hearted than at primary school, the pupils seemed less sanctimonious and less judgemental.

There was the fun of sports days and being at a top sports school, and the fun of Valentine's Day, when the art department produced cards for sale to be purchased by the lovelorn and the music students performed in the lovely garden on the western side of the quad during an extended lunch break. The Beatles' 'Eleanor Rigby' – *All the lonely people / Where do they all come from / All the lonely people* and Pete Seeger's 'Where have all the flowers gone?' always made it on to the playlist; why is anyone's guess. It left me with the lifelong impression that Valentine's Day was all about loneliness and missing flowers.

High school provided distractions from the stresses at home. I soon learnt to shut up about family, especially the pale family, even though I'm sure many of my classmates also had white family. I also censored myself on my uncool record collection. Nor did I mention the books I read after I'd been told off for reading a book on Israel's Six-Day War and the rule of Golda Meir.

We didn't speak about the removals, though many of the pupils were waiting to be removed from Claremont or my side of Lansdowne.

Now here's the thing: at high school, we switched from being the common garden variety term 'coloured' to using the infinitely more acceptable and hugely pretentious term 'so-called coloureds'. And when the latter was uttered, it had to be accompanied by air quotes. I didn't get what was wrong with just being coloured. A coloured is a coloured is a coloured.

When it came to political talk amongst the teen boys (the girls kept quiet), Ugandan dictator Idi Amin was the number-one subject, especially after he famously threatened to fly his fleet of MIG fighter jets to Cape Town and bomb the blitz out of the mountainside suburbs because that was where the whites lived.

In the newspapers and on the radio news Idi Amin was the bogeyman of choice in South Africa from 1971 to 1979. And as it turned out, in his country too, where his reign was brutal, cruel and oppressive. Its cost is still being counted today.

The boy-talk hit a high note when Idi Amin was said to have acquired a 6 000 kg giant white marble toilet, with pure gold fittings, shaped like the palm of a man's hand. It was believed to have been made in France and was modelled on Louis XVI's toilet, he who was dethroned and guillotined during the French Revolution of 1789. Had Idi Amin not heard of bad karma, I wondered.

The idea of the suite was that here was a big black backside pooping in a white hand. Why, I wondered again, were dictators so obsessed with toilets? Look at South Africa, even writing separate toilets into the law books. Freud and Jung might have had a field day with that question.

If Idi was the bogeyman to white South Africans and the subject of so-called coloured schoolboy jokes, then Muhammed Ali was the iconic black brother who 'floated like a butterfly and stung like a bee' and 'rumbled in the jungle'. For the boys in my class, Ali was the man to look up to. They really got their knickers in a knot about that brother. Ordinary teens did not know anything about Nelson Mandela and his Rivonia Trial friends, who after June 1964 simply ceased to exist in the heavily restricted local media.

We just heard rumours and rumours about rumours. They were disturbing. They distorted your thinking if you paid mind to them.

The written stories were certainly not available to read so that you could formulate your own opinion. The first time I heard about the African National Congress and the Pan Africanist Congress and all the other anti-apartheid organisations was at the University of the Western Cape in 1981. I knew about Steve Biko, though, because we held protests after it came to light that he had been murdered by police in September 1977.

Our teachers drummed into us the importance of critical thinking and to never take the news at face value. Read many sources of the news and formulate an opinion, we were told. And avoid reading the 'coloured rag' the *Cape Herald*. We had everything at home, so I read the much-maligned *Cape Herald* too. I even knew some of its reporters and one of its photographers.

At Livingstone High, Unity Movement teachers scoffed at any ideas of going to study at UWC, as they considered it to be a 'bush college' which couldn't possibly provide quality education. We all had to aspire to study at the University of Cape Town and were encouraged not to be put off by talk of the permits to do so.

The super-brainy were encouraged to think of studying in

157

England. We were urged to aim high. We had to 'Advance', as the school motto proclaimed – drummed into mushy teen minds in every Guidance class with Miss Carlier: *Nulla Vestige Retrorsum – No footsteps backwards.*

It was Miss Carlier who'd penned the lyrics of the school song, the refrain of which went 'We may roam the wide world over / we may stake our claim to wealth or fame / whatever end we seek / but we always will remember the school whose aim has been / *Nulla Vestige Retrorsum* / Livingstone our alma mater!'

Interesting set-work books in English, like the stories of Herman Charles Bosman, led me to take my reading up several notches. The school had a nice library on the first floor, with beautiful old bay windows that overlooked the quad and garden. I read Gerald Durrell's *My Family and Other Animals*, Harper Lee's *To Kill a Mockingbird*, John Howard's *Black like Me*, *The Diary of Anne Frank*, SE Hinton's *The Outsiders* and *That Was Then and This Is Now*, and JD Salinger's *The Catcher in the Rye*, to name a few.

At home, music-wise, I had graduated to Carole King's *Tapestry* and *Thoroughbred* LPs. Dear Carole had reminded so many in the world that: 'Now ain't it good to know that you've got a friend / When people can be so cold / They'll hurt you, yes, and desert you / And take your soul if you let them / Oh, but don't you let them'. And yes, Sister Carole, many heeded your words of consolation in times of darkness.

Later I also listened to the 'not kosher' white South African rock band Rabbitt, them of the song 'Charlie' from the *Boys Will Be Boys* LP fame . . . oops, yet another social gaffe.

Stella married Meneer Wilfie and he moved his wet-blanket personality into the master bedroom with her. Living in the tense atmosphere of Meneer Wilfie's moods was like playing Monopoly and the only card one could draw was the 'Go to jail' one.

In Ivan's book, the atmosphere was merely an invitation for him, Mavie, Dor and me to hit the road, sometimes to the top of Cavendish Square where there was a burger joint, like a drive-in set up. You pulled into a bay and a waiter or waitress on roller skates, all young whites, rolled up to the window and took your order. When we didn't go to this little-known mixed eatery, he drove to Rosmead Avenue in Claremont or Gabriel Road in Plumstead for Kentucky Fried Chicken. It went down well with fresh rolls from Coimbra Bakery on a Sunday evening. All of this was a bid to escape Meneer Wilfie's demeanour – and what a tasty escape it was too.

By 1975 I began my rescue mission of my amputated artist self: I found that I could make art out of words. This thought struck me after Mrs Newman, the English teacher, brought in her portable record player and played us Don McClean's song 'Vincent', about the famous artist Van Gogh. It was to teach us poetry.

My eyes were opened. I had another calling. If I was banned from painting pictures with paint, I would paint pictures with words. I began to write poetry. I fantasised that if I could get into art and geography class the following year, I could become a teacher of art, geography and also English. And that was quite something: the idea of teaching coming from a social misfit like me.

On the home front, we were stuck in the in-betweens of the goings and comings. From 1973 onwards the light had dimmed. A cloud of ever-present grey dust dulled the air as bulldozers demolished and builders constructed. Down the side streets, neat boxy houses were built for white people to move into.

I felt like the biblical 'left behind' – the story of the end-times

Mavie, Stella and Dor, 1992.

rapture as told in Matthew, where some are scooped off to heaven and others left behind on the fallen earth – as I watched new houses being built opposite where the familiar old ones once stood. Our new neighbours spoke mostly Afrikaans and had surnames like Du Pont, Steenkamp and Kotze – white people who came from unheard-of places beyond the Hex River.

While Mavie and the aunties were friendly towards the newcomers, they did not listen as attentively as they used to, either to them or to their old friends. They seemed distracted, their hearts heavy with uncertainty. Ivan became the main listener to others' stories.

With the addition of several dollops of white squeezed onto our palette of neighbourhood colours, the story pictures we were party to, changed. Soon the newcomers were making their way up the yard to speak to Ivan or coming in at the side gate (where the red parrot no longer held court) to tell Mavie of their woes and to use our bugged phone.

Family problems, I learnt, were not colour-coded. Everybody had their share of them. The new neighbours' dramas were more shocking in many ways: lots of divorce and stepchildren and exes and rage – and fear for the sons being sent to the military and to war. Army conscription was compulsory for white males and everyone had to go, usually at eighteen, just after completing school.

Two of the new houses across Dale Street had been built on property where one house had stood for at least 60 years. A prison warden couple – a brigadier, his wife and their son and daughter – lived in one of the houses. The Brigadier and Seun zeroed in on Ivan with his black-and-white Divisional Council Traffic Department squad car for chats. Not long after they moved in, Seun got his call-up and left for his basic army training. A few months later he came home, got married and disappeared shortly afterwards to the Angolan War.

The advent of TV with experimental programmes in mid-1975 brought welcome distraction. Meneer Wilfie bought a black-and-white Tedelex TV for the evening viewing slots. (There were only black-and-white sets available at first.) Apart from the ever-present test pattern and the singing of *Die Stem* at the close of viewing time, there were history documentaries, the children's program *Wielie Walie*, rugby, American sitcoms, such as *All in the family* and *The Partridge Family,* and variety shows.

One day Seun came back from Angola and didn't go again. He was a complete wreck, gaunt and nervous. He would visit Ivan some evenings and sit in a cane chair by the kitchen door, and every rustle of the leaves made him jump. The African Grey and the finches in their cages on the kitchen cupboard, Stella's new best buddies, had the same effect on him.

The proper military title for the war was The South African Border War, also known as The Angolan Bush War, which was fought across borders from then South West Africa into neighbouring Zambia and Angola, where the southern provinces were heavily mined. It was the South African Defence Force's (SADF) fight against the People's Liberation Army of Namibia (PLAN), the armed wing of the South West African People's Organisation (SWAPO). Taking the fight to southern Angola, the war entered into symbiosis with the Angolan Civil War and was part of the wars fought on the continuum of the decolonisation of Africa and the West's anti-communist Cold War with the Soviet-Cuban Block.

The conflict lasted from August 1966 to March 1990 and we all knew of the battles waged on the borders with the *rooi gevaar* – the communist threat. It was the main topic on the news, which provided carefully crafted propaganda. The *swart gevaar* or 'black threat' at the time paled in comparison in the public's imagination to the 'red threat', although it was an interwoven 'threat' as the liberation movement in exile had the backing of the Soviet Union and Cuba, where combatants received their political and military training.

Apartheid had many layers and each layer had points of attack and counterattack. Some of those points were considered soft or on-going low impact conflict, like the slow dripping of a faulty tap, an irritant. We lived in a country at war, a country that did not acknowledge the majority as citizens – just incidentals with the potential to be enemies. So was it our war too, or were we just part of the irritant droplets coming out of the faulty tap in the backyard?

These questions caused problems for those who could not switch off and get on with life, tra-la-la-la. Get a safe job at the bank, an insurance company, the City Council, a big company. Be a nurse, be a teacher, meet the right people, fall in love, marry, buy a house, have babies, worry a bit about whether to pack for Perth or Toronto, or stay here and cheat on the wife, get a divorce and be a show-off starting all over again with a new woman. Hamsters on a wheel in a cage.

Ivan, who didn't have much time for Christianity, took to muttering darkly that we lived in a God-forsaken land. Years later he sent me a postcard advising me to get out of Mitchells Plain because it was a God-forsaken place.

At the end of 1975, we went on our one and only camping holiday 'while we still have time' before the removal, not knowing what the future held for us. We appeared to be running out of time very fast. Ivan, Mavie, Dor and I loaded Ivan's crock Ford Taunus and went on a tour of the Southern Cape for a week after Christmas. Although there were rondavels at the Mossel Bay and Kleinkrans camping sites, we camped in a tent. Non-whites weren't allowed to stay in hotels.

From there we went to Knysna and the Cango Caves at Oudtshoorn. The furthest we got was Plettenberg Bay on a day trip.

It was very beautiful, but the memories of holidays fade, no matter how much you promise yourself that you will never forget what you have convinced yourself is the ultimate life-enhancing moment.

The dissembling

THE TURNING POINT came in 1976. The year started with the usual removals, bulldozing and building, but then something changed.

In Heatherley Road, the house began to look like a furniture warehouse, as Ivan and Mavie sourced dining room furniture at the antique store next to La Scala Bioscope on Claremont Main Road and kitchen furniture from elsewhere.

They'd paid a deposit on a house at 62 Ajax Way, Woodlands in Mitchells Plain. The area was to consist of about 200 houses with plots measuring 420 square metres each. The area bordered on Philippi farms that were still operational.

As a traffic officer with the Divisional Council, Ivan would benefit from the Council's housing subsidy. They were finally going to do this thing – move – before they were told to *fokoff*.

Moving had been on the cards from late 1975. We went a few times to the City Council visitors' centre and the fully furnished model house situated in Westridge, Mitchells Plain where the first houses in the first suburb in the new city for coloureds were being built.

The area was modelled on European housing estates and consisted mostly of townhouses and ranch-style houses with small front gardens. It was quite lovely, all new and clean. Ivan also took family and friends who were on the brink of removal to view the development. But the area was not to Ivan and Mavie's taste, although I always thought that we would have done well there. Knowing their propensity for running around, the Westridge houses which were built closer together would have been much better for lock-up-and-go. But they chose Woodlands.

Ivan and Mavie were very excited. They researched curtaining and carpets. In Lansdowne, the old sash windows were dressed as they always had been: nets and long curtains with the tops hidden under pelmets. In Mitchells Plain, the window frames would be metal, and wide rather than long. They eventually found out that if they bought curtaining, rails and Kirsch prongs at Greatermans at Cavendish Square, they could have their curtains made up and fitted too. Yes, that's what they would do.

With the house buying came talk of property insurance and life insurance policies and the worry suddenly about what they would do when it came to death. Neither wanted to be buried, so they went along for a tour of the Maitland Crematorium that they saw advertised in the *Cape Times*. The City Council was worried about running out of space at cemeteries and had embarked on a campaign to educate people about cremation.

My parents' graphic and unrestrained talk about these things left me with a new worry: being orphaned. It's no wonder that I suffered from Adrenal Fatigue Syndrome long before doctors and scientists identified it. They were like AA Milne's Rabbit and Tigger to my Eeyore and Owl. I would still be contemplating whether I should put my left foot or my right foot forward to reach the door and they would be right at the end of the driveway, beckoning me to hurry up.

My ponderousness irritated Stella no end and one day when

they rushed ahead of me on the walk down Garfield Road to Kenilworth Centre, she commented to Mavie, as if I could not hear, 'She's not like you or Ivan'. It stung. Such comments always did. Many others in their circle had the same complaint. Individuality was just *so* undesirable.

It was also 'selfish'. The acceptable position seemed to be, 'We must stand together as a community and give up our brains and our ability to think, see and hear. We must not form opinions of our own, only fawn over a few half-baked and largely unfounded comments from dodgy old men and conceited young lads. Feeling is desirable, of course – the more dramatic the better – because we all need to be entertained.'

Drama has always been grist for the mill for petty people.

I survived the crippling and rather unfair prejudging and criticism, bone-weary though I usually was. After all those years seeking to escape school, I had reached a plateau of acceptance about it. I was fourteen-and-a-half and in Standard 8 and again I had asked to be shifted to the art and geography classes. Again my request was turned down.

I stopped trying at German and maths. I sunk all my energies into English. At the same time, in Afrikaans second language, I enjoyed our prescribed set-work book: Uys Krige's journeys in Spain in *Sol Y Sombra* and in France in *Vêr in die wêreld*. In English we were studying Laurie Lee's non-fiction books, *Cider with Rosie* and *As I walked out one midsummer morning*. Those travel stories captured my imagination. They made up for not being allowed to study geography.

We met Shakespeare in the run-up to the end of school days. It was the great big fear that his plays we studied in English would be too difficult to comprehend. I saw my first Shakespearean play that year – *Julius Caesar* at Maynardville in Wynberg with Mavie, Ivan, Dor, Granny Davids and Aunty Doreen. I didn't say anything about it at school because I wasn't sure if theatre was one of the places to boycott or not.

Same when I went a year or two later to see Aunty Doreen in a play at the Baxter. She played a French maid in a Peter Krummeck production. Aunty Doreen loved Shakespeare, but she was a Francophile too and later on studied French at the Alliance Française at the Town Centre in Mitchells Plain. Claude Debussy's song *Clair De Lune* was her favourite, she once told me, and on her bookshelves were some French classics like Gustave Flaubert's *Madame Bovary* and Victor Hugo's *Les Misérables*. Of course, those shelves were chock-full of Shakespeare, also *Far from the Madding Crowd* by Thomas Hardy and his *Tess of the D'Urbervilles*. The only modern book was Colleen McCullough's *The Thorn Birds*. She insisted I read the book which is set in Australia, a place she'd visited on holiday and had loved.

Classics and language and Shakespeare and God and flowers and cake and tea and who the heck needed to be boxed in by apartheid? The mind could take you places where the cumbersome could not follow.

From my studies of *Julius Caesar,* the line that has stayed with me is Marc Antony's: 'I come to bury Caesar, not to praise him. The evil that men do lives after them; The good is oft interred with their bones'.

I was never interested in 'Friends, Romans and Countrymen' lending me their ears. I had nothing to say to anyone. I still think of that line when I find myself in uncomfortable and unwelcoming situations. It has come to mean, 'Let's just get this over and done with and get the hell out of here.'

My silly little teenage concerns about my future were nothing compared to the importance of moving to a new house. Like soldiers in the army, we had to live lives ahead of ourselves, hurrying up and waiting. The waiting brought brittleness, boredom and restlessness. Waiting meant frittering away time, nit-picking, being petty and short-tempered. It bore holes in your life, never to be refilled with usefulness again.

I found the dying days of apartheid about twelve years later to be the same. Change was about to happen, but there was no way of knowing from which direction it would come.

Around the time that Mavie, Ivan and I were packing boxes to leave Lansdowne, the long, long protest march to end apartheid entered the public consciousness. There were student body protests throughout the country following the Soweto uprising of 16 June 1976 against Bantu education and the enforced use of Afrikaans as the language of instruction. Livingstone High, situated just a few metres from the newly built Claremont Police Station, joined the march.

At most coloured high schools, the pupils held placard demonstrations inside school grounds. At ours, we sang Joan Baez protest songs taught to us by the student leaders as we marched around the school: 'We shall overcome, we shall overcome, we shall overcome, someday. Oh, deep in my heart, I do believe, we shall overcome, someday.' There was one about 'Freedom isn't free', but I've forgotten the rest of the lyrics.

We stood in silence on our side of the fence all around from Lansdowne Road to the Second Avenue side of the school. Our placards and banners were made by the art students. On the pavement side of the fence, opposite us, the cops lined up with their guns with looks on their young faces that seemed to be saying, 'I'd rather be loafing around the station, doing *fokkol*.'

The white businesses near the school were jittery because of our presence in the area and closed early on the first day of protests. But we were mild-mannered *sissies* and didn't resort to destroying or looting neighbouring businesses. Being a bunch of lah-di-dah 'so-called coloureds' bound for UCT, we would not resort to plebeian vulgarities such as breaking windows and stealing.

We did not experience the beatings and teargas and arrests that the township high schools experienced in most of the major cities and towns throughout 1976. Eventually, the national education department closed the schools for a few days, just before the end of the quarter. I could live with not going to school.

In the third quarter, there were intermittent days of protest. Elsewhere, the scenes were violent. This we could still see on the TV news and in the newspapers, while in the 1980s the State of Emergency laws would severely censor the news.

While Dor, Stella and Meneer Wilfie stayed on in the family house, still without a clue about what they would do next, we moved east to Mitchells Plain. I was fifteen. I had never lived in a home with just three people in it. I was now in a nuclear family.

Brigadier and Seun came to fit burglar bars and gates for our new house which they welded in their garage in Dale Street. These were a first for us, but it was better to be safe than sorry, was the rationale.

The truth is, we were all afraid. We lived in unknown, semi-rural territory among people who were strangers. To the north, on the western side of Duinefontein Road, there were gangsters galore in Manenberg and Hanover Park, running into Athlone.

Mavie and Ivan's house at 62 Ajax Way, Woodlands, Mitchells Plain, 1993.

And on the eastern side of the road, there was rioting, teargas and birdshot in the black townships.

We had to pass those areas to get to the turn-off to Mitchells Plain at Weltevreden Road. It felt like we were living on a different planet entirely, one I never really trusted or fully adjusted to. I suspect that is where my put-a-smile-on-the-dial and soldier-on mentality came from. It helped me – until the day I crashed out.

Ivan and Mavie threw themselves into home décor and gardening. Their months of planning were coming to fruition. They were also playing catch-up in creating their own identity, one away from the family dynamic of Heatherley. It was a novelty to them, something new and exciting, like going to see an opera.

Because there was no public transport to Woodlands, I didn't move fully to the new house. I stayed on in Lansdowne during the week and only went home weekends. In Dor's room, where my bed had stood for as long as I could remember, I slept on the fold-up camp bed that had always been used for visitors.

Without Mavie there to come home to in the afternoons, the house was a cold, sad, lifeless space. No fire burning in the stove, no smell of cooking.

After school, I used to walk around with my friends in Claremont and then I'd go to the old library near Station Road, before going home in the late afternoon. I always went alone to the library, because the others lived within walking distance of Lansdowne Library. I would read the excerpts from novels in the textbooks *English Today* and *English Alive*. When I found a writing style or a story that appealed to me, I would go to the library to find the books.

That's how I found Francoise Sagan's *Bonjour Tristesse*. It fascinated and inspired me, knowing that the book had been published when she was just eighteen years old. I tried to find more of her books, but there was only that one on the shelves in the young adult section. I was not brave enough to venture to the adult shelves. I tried to find *Memoirs of a Dutiful Daughter* by Simone de Beauvoir, but I could never locate it in any of the main city libraries I looked in. When I was fact-checking for this book, I was pleased to see that it is now available as an e-book. The excerpt I read captivated me and I want to know the rest of the story.

When I got to Woodlands on Fridays, Mavie would be waiting with news of the people they had met. For the first time, she was telling only me her stories. I'd graduated from being the tin soldier she had to sergeant-major to hustle through life, into a mostly tuned-out little sister with ornaments for ears. She wanted to hear my stories from school and I was obliged to tell them.

The house was clean, comfortable and pleasant. The main bedroom was about four by four-and-a-half square metres and had one big window and one small window on the side. I had the room at the back. It was light and airy. I'd brought along Great-grandma Minnie's oak dressing table, which had come from Great-grandpa José's Lawson-Road house, and an oak kitchen chair I found on the stoep. This was my new desk set-up. I still had the same bed and cupboard I'd always had.

The lounge and my backroom also had two windows each. The middle room was where Ivan created a studio and study for himself. He had a draughtsman's table, a desk and his easel and paints all set up in there.

The house was spacious and light poured in. It spread over more than 120 square metres and had a garage and a large garden. For the first time, we had a lawn. There were many firsts that year.

My parents made friends, but they soon found out that their taste in friends were completely incompatible. Ivan went for the brittle, disparaging kind of party people. He didn't see that his teetotalling self was being taken for a *gek*, a joke.

Mavie didn't trust that sort of person. She gravitated towards the humble and kind women from the church who hosted priests from Lansdowne for services in their homes. Or towards the women in our road – the sort Ivan's party types would ignore.

I drifted. Home had always been a smallholding in the middle of a suburban neighbourhood, and then suddenly it wasn't anymore and there was no freedom to ponder nature without the ever-present fear of attack, and I could no longer lift my hand in the familiar garden and pick a fruit to eat, even though you had to watch where you bite because there were worms in most of the fruit. As the removals moved closer, the worms proliferated. A sort of final hooray.

I missed home. The colours, the flowers, the trees, the plants, the birds – the people who came and went. I was there in the Heatherley Road home that was no longer home during the week and it reminded me constantly of what I had lost.

But I had books and music. And I made an effort to find beauty.

I found it in the quality of the light and the air, especially in winter when the farmlands became waterlogged vleis the birds visited in large numbers. In spring, there was the blooming of the humble veld flowers to witness. These things had a lyrical beauty to them.

Ivan still did the scenic-view driving and the keeping up of traditions, but the magic and texture had seeped out of them. On some occasions, at the end of a long day of being a tourist about the Peninsula, Ivan would round it off with a drive to the top of Signal Hill. Or at the other end of the mountain range, going to Boyes Drive, Ou Kaapse Weg or Red Hill for the view of the lights coming on.

From there it was a long way back to Mitchells Plain, before the highways and broad boulevards were built to cut off the en-visioned coloured homeland in times of trouble. We had to travel through the lush, still fully functioning, stinking-of-animal-manure Philippi farmlands.

It seemed a full moon would always be shining through the tall blue gum trees along the Neu Eisleben farm track that led to Woodlands. To compound the spooky effects – and my jitters – Ivan would recite, 'The Highwayman' by Alfred Noyes: 'The wind was a torrent of darkness among the gusty trees. / The moon was a ghostly galleon tossed upon cloudy seas. / The road was a ribbon of moonlight over the purple moor, / And the highwayman came riding— / Riding—riding—.'

As if the constant fear of Ivan's car breaking down wasn't enough, when we reached home (before the time of streetlights, tarred roads and Highlands Drive) there would be an owl sitting on our front wall. My conclusion was we were doomed.

I made an effort to make friends, or rather, Ivan or Mavie made the effort to make friends for me. One weekend I came home and they had befriended the people who lived two houses away. The Heynes family had moved from District Six. My impression of them was that all they did on weekends was cook curries and rotis and sit in their lounge, eating, drinking whisky and talking about District Six. From knowing nothing about District Six before, we learned about every nook and cranny of the place through them.

Mrs Heynes had two daughters, Shirley and Michelle. We sometimes hung out, talked about music and whatever was the topic of the day. Sometimes we'd hit the road and go places outside of Mitchells Plain.

Visitors still found their way to Woodlands, taking a few wrong turns. As always, they pitched unannounced. Dor came to visit us every Sunday and stayed over for public holidays, so we never really lost touch with Lansdowne. In November, the old friends visited for Ivan's birthday. On New Year's Day, everybody turned up for Mavie's birthday. A few of our new neighbours were also invited. The traditions continued.

I failed Standard 8 at the end of 1976. No surprise. I hadn't tried to pass at all. I was not going back to Livingstone anyway and would transfer to the newly built Westridge High School in 1977. I lasted there four days before I asked to go back to Livingstone. I wouldn't be staying in Lansdowne during the week any-more though. I would commute. Morning lifts were organised with neighbours Mr and Mrs Weber as far as Wynberg and I would travel to Claremont from there.

In the afternoons I would go from Claremont to Duinefontein Road, the entry road to Manenberg, taking either the Manenberg or Crossroads bus. I would cross Lansdowne Road to Weltevreden Road to the only bus stop for Mitchells Plain. The bus ran from Manenberg to Westridge. It was tricky to get to the bus stop on time so as not to miss the single ride home in the afternoon.

Initially, Mavie would walk alone up the long and dusty farm track lined with blue gum trees to meet me. It was enjoyable in a way, living in the country and walking through the fields. We sel-dom saw people on Neu Eisleben Road and nothing untoward ever happened. It was about a kilometre and a half into Wood-lands. Every day I sang John Denver's song: 'Country Road take me home, to a place I belong . . .'

Soon other schoolkids, three from Oaklands High in Lans-downe and one from Livingstone, moved into the area and we'd all meet up at the bus stop at Weltevreden Road and walk in together, relieving Mavie of her chaperone duties.

As time went by, when we missed the bus, the Livingstone girl – Shirley Lawrence, who was also in Standard 8 – and I would hitch rides as far as the farm track. Again, nothing ever happened to us. We just wanted to get home after those long, often unpleas-ant bus rides from Claremont.

I became a bullshitter during those years, with the capacity to talk myself and whoever was with me out of any tricky situa-tion. I had learnt to fake – just to get through and not get stuck in what I was convinced was not a good place to be in.

Everything felt like a long journey to another country. The sights were seen, the people were met, but there came that time when there was a longing to get back to my real life, to catch a plane for home. Only there was no such thing. It was still there, but Lansdowne wasn't my home anymore.

In a new class in my repeat of Standard 8, I was able to get out of German but not maths. German was replaced with history. There were lots of Germans in history, three years of Germans at war, getting the crap shot out of them by the Allies. I could live with history and I did reasonably well in the subject. It was a chance for me to use my burgeoning writing skills. It was still a 'no' to the switching to art and geography, though.

Shakespeare was back to befuddle and test limited teen vocabularies in *The Merchant of Venice*. Along with thousands of other Standard 8s wherever they found themselves, I puzzled over Portia's speech to a Venetian Court, 'The quality of mercy is not strained. / It droppeth as the gentle rain from heaven / Upon the place beneath: It is twice blest; / It blesseth him that gives and him that takes.'

The year meandered along.

Then 1978 brought more startling changes.

Meneer Wilfie and Stella announced that they had bought a house from a family emigrating to Canada and would move early in the year. Dor would stay on at the old house, she said, until Grandpa Jack decided what to do with it.

She wasn't there alone for long before Grandpa Jack returned home to live on the studio couch in the lounge. The couch was less than two metres from the sideboard where Great-grandpa Joe's Bible stood and a black-and-white photo of Grandma Florie holding newborn me with my crown of thorns. There were three empty rooms in the house, but the lounge was where he wanted to be.

He had Alzheimer's disease. He constantly ran away from Miss Lizzie's house in Belgravia Estate where they'd been living since their marriage in 1965. Like a homing pigeon, he would walk from there, cross busy main roads, walk under the subway at Crawford, and make his way to Dale Street.

One weekend he came to stay with us in Woodlands and decided he wanted to live with us. Mavie said no. She didn't want to look after him. She and Ivan made sure to give him a good scrubbing and proper shave though, because with his illness he failed to wash. His sons, Uncle Kenny, Uncle Joey and Uncle Johnny, also pitched in to help keep the old man clean.

At the old house, Dor had to get help to look after him during the day while she was at work. Uncle Johnny's wife Aunty Bertha from Bridgetown came to stay. And when she wasn't around, Mrs Eksteen from next door in one of the wood-and-iron houses in Lee-Pan's yard, or Meneer Wilfie's mother Mrs Coetzee would stay with him. Once Grandpa returned to Lansdowne though, he never ran away again.

I continued to travel by bus with Shirley from high school. We made the long journey fun for ourselves. More schoolmates had moved to Mitchells Plain, which was growing steadily suburb by suburb.

Granny Davids and Aunty Doreen moved to Portlands, Mitchells Plain, ending more than forty years at 30 Chichester Road, Claremont. More and more family and former neighbours moved to the coloured city. Those who had been forcefully removed to places like Hanover Park and Manenberg were now able to buy their own homes and leave the townships behind.

The joke doing the rounds about Mitchells Plain was that we drank water recycled from sewage – the City Council had built state-of-the-art sewage works at Rocklands and that was evidence enough that there was something dodgy about our water. My over-active imagination made up a story that connected the bad behaviour I saw around me to the quality of the water. I never once considered that it could be environmental strain.

Then there was the joke about us being so poor, we hung Joko tea bags on the washing line after visitors had been, to dry out for reuse when they visited again.

It wasn't half as bad as the joke about moving to Fairways. 'A woman was busy ironing in her kitchen. She heard a window break and discovered a burglar putting his hand through the window. With iron aloft she burnt the hand, sending the burglar yelping away in pain. The next day she saw her neighbour and noted that his hand was bandaged in the same spot where she had burnt the burglar.'

These silly stories and jokes stuck in my head for a long time. I struggled to understand the need for them. I wouldn't let them go until I could find a plausible reason for these types of tales. Was it for entertainment, or was there some hidden meaning I was missing?

The political cognoscenti had great disdain for the coloured homeland of Mitchells Plain. Even the Imams at the Mosque expressed dubiousness, especially about the water there. We had only one Muslim family in our part of Ajax Way. There were certainly fewer than ten Muslim families in those first two years of Woodlands – called Old Woodlands these days.

No gangsters were congregating on the corners. It was an isolated area. But the stigma about living in the 'wrong areas' was well underway. People in the more upmarket areas, or who were closer to the business hubs made a habit of shaming people from townships or Mitchells Plain. The way I was seeing things, *schadenfreude* was one of those negative behaviours that soon became a cornerstone of the customary Cape Town condition. Widely known as to 'gorra' or to 'gwarra', people insult and mock others in the form of a joke that the person receiving is expected to take in good humour and with grace. I couldn't understand it. An address was just an address, a physical location on a map. It didn't make you the person you were or might become later. What was all that bullshit about staying the same, anyway? People change, became healthier or slip into a downward spiral. They grow into themselves, become their own person.

School continued as usual. My Standard 9 class, based in the Physics Lab Room 4, consisted of more than 24 boys and six girls. My break-time hang-out buddies were fellow uncool teens Trevor, Jitendra, Kulsum and Pam.

The other friends, from my first three years at high school, were in matric now and headed to UCT to study. They were mostly girls and they were off to study science and medicine. That was the great thing about Livingstone: when it came to brainpower and academics, the playing fields were level and everybody was treated equally. Those girls were all so solid and neat and focused. I wondered how they knew what direction to take, how to concentrate, and how to envisage a future. I remember how head girl Carlyn, who went on to become a doctor (and who sadly died of cancer in 1990), looked at us one day and said she could see everybody's futures mapped out before them: the teachers, scientists, journalists, oral hygienists. She said that they would all have families of their own. But when she looked at me, she said she could see nothing. Just a blank space.

It was true. I had always been unscripted, like a joker in the deck with zero value, until a value was attributed so that the game could proceed.

When it came to politics, the boys were more vociferous in my new class, which was wilder than my previous class had been. Discussions would be so heated, boys might come to blows. One day Kader even took a swipe at Keith with a penknife. Our class was always in trouble for noisiness because the boys nattered endlessly – and we would all be marched to the principal's office for a *skelling*.

From those boys, I learnt about Mr Hassan Howa's SACOS (South African Council on Sport) and their refusal to play sport with white teams. SACOS led the field in campaigning to have white South Africa's teams boycotted by the international sporting community. The boycott campaign slogan was 'No normal sport in an abnormal society'. Boycotting playing in multi-racial teams or matches was a matter of following the tradition of principled opposition to racism in the Western Cape.

I was growing my writing skills, and I often used my travels to and from school as grist for my mill. I no longer drove with the neighbours to Wynberg in the mornings but travelled by bus from Woodlands to Manenberg. I changed on Manenberg Avenue to the Claremont bus. It would still be dark while I waited there with adults on their way to work. I wrote compositions about those shadowy early-morning figures.

Those misty mornings had a soundtrack.

Perhaps it was the proximity to Sherwood Park, where Pacific Express performed as the resident band at the lounge for many years, but the soundtrack that played in the dilly-day-dreams teen head of mine was Zane Adam and Pacific Express's 'Give a little love'. It was blended in with Chicago's 'Just you 'n' me': 'Won't you give a little love this time, you are my love and my life, you are my inspiration, just you and me to carry on, simple and free, yesterday's gone away . . .' And there was a full brass section playing in my head: Jimmy Pankow and Walter Parazaider blasting up a storm with Robbie Jansen and Basil Manenberg Coetzee.

After my compositions on Manenberg saw the light of dawn, English teacher Mr Peter Fiske, who taught us the great writing device of using mind maps, asked if I would consider entering the English Olympiad held at Grahamstown every year. I said neither yes nor no, just nodded my head, because it was not often that a teacher spoke to me other than to correct or *skel*. The boys had been listening in and came over to verify what Mr Fiske said to me. I told them and they informed me, rather brusquely, 'You can't go. We don't participate in anything organised by the whites. Our society is not normal, so we can't compete with them.'

I'd been thinking about studying journalism at Grahamstown and had brochures at home. And even though I knew that Ivan, whose most ambitious dream for me was to get an office job, wouldn't let me attend university, it would have been nice to see the campus for myself. Mr Fiske's belief that I was good enough to compete was a real psychological boost for me, as those boosts were few and far between.

I continued to write. In my maths books, where there should have been theorems, there was poetry. At the beginning of the year, as always, Ivan took me to see deputy principal Mr Dudley at his home and I asked, same as every year, to change to art and geography. As always, the answer was no. I simply asked as a matter of principle every year, because I wanted to change more than anything, but I knew the nature of the beast and that I would be shot down. It was a game to them, I think.

Ivan and me – we were never going to see eye to eye. He had faith in fakes and worshipped charlatans.

I felt set up. By teachers, by priests, by adults. I had been programmed to think in school – first I had a solid grounding in church and primary school and then high school was based on analysis, fact, logic and empiricism – and yet with Ivan, I had to endure all kinds of esoterisms. It sure as hell smelled like crap, that nasty incense he brought home to 'cleanse his aura' with.

I felt robbed of light and fresh air while he took part in what I saw as irrational rituals. At school, we were encouraged to move forward, not backward, and here I was being subjected to delusional superstition. No one could just back-step when they had built up years of learning and training the brain to think and reason.

Cousin Thomas, who made a life of making proclamations on the state of the family, said the Davids family was 'divided into those who were superstitious and those who were suspicious'. For once I agreed with him.

I despaired of ever finding a future, only I didn't have the knowledge or the words to define my uneasiness. There was just something very strange and very wrong with all these mysterious rituals and practices.

Mavie and me, we talked, bickered, traded witticisms, took pot-shots and joked. Sometimes there would be an epic mutual *skelling* like the ones she used to have with Uncle Joey. By my mid-teens, I went round for round with her. And then we'd start talking again after a while. Quick flash tempers might release tension, but they don't solve the real problems bubbling beneath the surface.

It was in those years that Mavie first started telling me stories about the past, the ones that form the basis of this book. When we lived in Lansdowne, the tales I gathered were mostly what I overheard. I wasn't gathering the family stories with intent – I simply heard them and puzzled over the particulars. And they stuck.

In October 1978, Grandpa Jack died. Mavie, the aunties, Miss Lizzie and a few others were at his couch-side. While he was sick, the Catholic priests visited him and he converted to receive the sacraments such as communion, sacraments for the sick and finally the sacrament for the dying.

The funeral was held at Our Lady Help of Christians Church and burial was at the family plot at Klip Cemetery. It was a huge funeral, with all his children present, and his friends, and family from everywhere they had wandered over the years. It was the last big gathering at the house that Great-grandpa Joe had built.

I remember it being a terrible time for the family. Uncle Joey, Grandpa Jack's oldest son, died two months later, in the week between Christmas and New Year. It was a devastating blow for everyone, as sudden deaths always are, especially for Aunty

Aunty Dorothy, Stella and Mavie on a picnic at Wynberg Park, 2003.

Dorothy and his children and grandchildren. Mavie was inconsolable, a keening grieving that she never had with Grandpa Jack's passing. Ivan's family too, Granny Davids and Aunty Doreen – whom Uncle Joey liked and often visited when he was working in that part of Claremont when they still lived there – were shocked and deeply saddened.

Matric 1979 began in sadness. Cousin Lee-Lee started that year at Livingstone in Standard 7, still very sad about Uncle Joey, her grandfather.

That year, Standards 10C and D were mixed up – some of our class went to theirs and vice versa. Our friend Trevor was among the removed, but we still saw him when they came over for history and physics and our new classmates went over to their old class. We had to study hard and pass exams and ponder the future and be as optimistic as could be. Life went on. It always does.

The high school programme followed its usual pattern. First, there was inter-house sports day, usually held at Rosmead Sports Field, where the entire student body was divided into houses: red, green, yellow and blue. The athletes competed and the school team was chosen from first-, second- and third-place winners in every event.

The inter-school sports day was held at Athlone Stadium and was the highlight of the school year. There was also a swimming gala day, when everybody walked, class by class, down Rosmead Avenue to the swimming pool in Wynberg. Sport was a serious business and considered a unifying element.

During the school's annual winter inter-class 'mini world tournament', an event to motivate pupils to participate in healthy activities, our matric class of 'radicals' decided to be the USSR. The removed boys in 10D were still part of our class team and one boy got his mom to make the flag. She sewed it perfectly and appliqued the yellow hammer, sickle and star on the red material. It was then proudly displayed on the back wall of our lab class.

About midway through the tournament, we received an unexpected visitor. We were diligently working through our textbooks, silent for a change, when there was a knock on the door. A white police officer with brass on his epaulettes walked in and nodded a greeting at the teacher. He went right to the back of the class, snatched the flag off the wall, and marched out again.

That our class flag had been confiscated by the police caused quite a buzz throughout the school. When it came to the final day of the tournament, the team marched without the flag. What a drama. It was hilarious too, that a bunch of school kids playing winter sports could get that kind of reaction from the police.

How did they know? Who informed them?

But we had more to worry about than what apartheid was getting up to with its rah-rah look-at-me attitude.

We had Shakespeare to shake things up, for instance. In Standard 9 we'd been encouraged to attend the matinee performance of *Hamlet* at Spes Bona Boys High in Athlone, even though we weren't doing Shakespeare in that year. The Bard could make or break your English results – that's how powerful he was.

That year we had other literary heavyweights to wrestle with: George Eliot's *Silas Marner* and Arthur Miller's *The Crucible*. Literature shows you, through the beauty of language, the many aspects of the human condition: suffering, sadness, injustice, oppression. When you're young, it sweeps you away. You work yourself up about it and fail to see that the authors have subtly woven into their tales more than one way out of the dire situations they have dreamed up for their characters. Oddly enough, it felt to me that the teens of my generation had hope during those days, in spite of the fact that our education had been designed by the authorities to dumb us down. We were second class. Our equipment and resources were sub-standard.

I remember Spes Bona's *Hamlet* performance of 1978 well. We travelled by bus from Claremont to Thornton Road and then walked the rest of the way to the school, near the N2. Turfhall Road hadn't been broadened into a dual carriageway, nor had Jan Smuts Drive been constructed.

The stage on which Hamlet delivered his famous 'To be or not to be' soliloquy was not a fancy one. The Shakespeare plays reflected for me so much of the society I found myself a member of.

As the night watchman Marcellus in *Hamlet* commented, 'Something is rotten in the state of Denmark.' We may not have been in Denmark in fifteen-*voetsak*, but it was obvious to those with eyes in their heads that many things were rotten in the state of here.

In matric, we studied *Antony and Cleopatra*. The lines that stood out the most for me were uttered by Enobarbus, on the state of Antony and Cleopatra's illicit liaison, 'Age cannot wither, nor custom stale / Her infinite variety. Other women cloy / The appetites they feed, but she makes hungry / Where most she satisfies, for vilest things / Become themselves to her, that the holy priests / Bless her when she is riggish.'

Over the years, I've often thought how ahead of his time Shakespeare was. Good ol' Will spoke of feminism and liberation when mankind was 'everywhere in chains'.

I often wonder whether that was why Aunty Doreen was so drawn to Shakespeare. Perhaps she dreamt of being something other than a dutiful coloured daughter-sister-aunt in her family and inspiring teacher to the young children she taught at primary schools in Steenberg. What would she have chosen for herself, other than a life of duty?

All the commuter to-and-fro-ing of my last school years used up a lot of brainpower that should have gone into doing well academically. I just got by, reserving my greatest energies for English and history and cruising through the rest. Or not, as was the case with maths.

The Golden Arrow bus service, which covered the Mitchells Plain route, made Hanover Park the exchange hub. Shirley, a few other schoolmates and I travelled to Hanover Park on Tramways buses and changed to the Mitchells Plain bus there. The bus would exit off Weltevreden Road, travel in a loop through Westridge as far as Rocklands, then back north through the newer parts of Westridge and Woodlands, all the way to the end of the road, which was at the newly built Woodlands High School.

We parted ways there. Shirley went to her section of Ajax Way and I walked towards Highlands Drive, which was in the process of being upgraded into the carriageway it is today. There was an embankment between it and Ajax Way, and the Council had planted a neat row of Norfolk pine trees.

From those first few houses in 1976, Mitchells Plain had grown quickly on many fronts, all the way to the coast, and further eastward. Not all the residents were recently removed from the suburbs. Some came from families who'd been removed in the 1950s when they were still children. As adults, they were buying their first homes in which to raise their families. They wanted their own homes, and they wanted to get out of the townships. Others came from country towns or from the Southern and Eastern Cape to the much-touted 'model city' for coloureds.

For the 'common people', it was disturbing to be left so naked in public, so people clothed themselves in sophistry. They wove webs of false argument and huddled together – misplaced as their ancestors had been once, from whatever corner of the world they'd been spirited away from. For many, the forced removals were the ultimate wake-up call.

During the three years of becoming dislodged from my previous life – from July 1976 to 1979 – I read my way through a blur of books that included George Orwell's *Animal Farm* and Robert Pirsig's *Zen and the Art of Motorcycle Maintenance*. Also, five books that came highly recommended by classmates: Henri Charriere's *Papillon* and *Banco*, Nicky Cruz' *The Cross and the Switchblade* and *Run Baby Run* and Frederick Forsyth's *Day of the Jackal*. I listened my way through Chicago, Joan Baez, Jethro Tull, Pacific Express, Boz Scaggs, James Taylor, Santana, The Doors, The Eagles' *Hotel California*, America's *Horse with no name*, Emmy Lou Harris, Janis Ian, Queen, and always Carole King.

While I waited for the matric results, reading music reviews in *The Weekend Argus* one Saturday, I came across a Zen aphorism in an article: *The weight of living is as heavy as a mountain, death is as light as a feather.* The words stuck in my mind as it seemed to sum up what I had seen, for many years living so close to the mountain.

From toddlerhood, I had been taught to revere that mountain at the end of the Lansdowne Road. I knew where every track was. I knew every member of my family's stories about their days of climbing the mountain. I'd climbed the mountain many times with them too. But I did not love that mountain at the end of the road as much as my family, especially Mavie, did.

I learnt to look at the mountain to see whether it would rain or not that day. If the colour was a dark slate, when it looked 'really angry', as Dor used to say, it was going to pour buckets. If the cloud cover was low, you could see the rainfall over Newlands, and soon the clouds would move east to pour buckets. I looked out for mountain streams in winter, as I had been taught. I knew that Maclear's Beacon was the highest point with its elevation of 1 086 metres above sea level.

I remembered the spot where a Mirage fighter jet of the South African Airforce had slammed into Devil's Peak in the vicinity of the blockhouse. There was a scar on the mountain for a long time afterwards.

The mountain became the subject of recurring nightmares for at least two decades. I used to dream that I had to crawl up the mountain, but the top, where the dams are, was always out of reach. I'd wake up trembling. It felt like the dreams were a warning, but I didn't know what they were warning me against.

As the decade drew to an anxious close, I became comfortably numb in Pink Floyd's company. My matric results arrived. I'd surpassed myself in mediocrity, except for a B in English.

And then it was no more

IN LANSDOWNE Grandpa Jack's estate had to be wound up and that was in the hands of a lawyer in Athlone.

As soon as Grandpa's death notice appeared in the newspapers, Dor received a visit from one of the white Volksie officials with the newspaper clipping in hand. She referred him to the lawyer. They delivered an ultimatum to the lawyer: Now that the owner was deceased, the property had to be sold.

While the lawyer negotiated with the officials, Dor stayed another year alone in the old house. She read the Bible or worked in the garden, read books on crafts and flower arranging, or fed stray neighbourhood cats that had moved into the vacated chicken run. On Sundays, she came to visit us.

As I was writing this, I wondered how it felt to come home to the big old house that would soon be emptied of all remaining furniture and decades of accumulated stuff. How long did it take her to light the fire in the stove and get it going? Did she even have the energy to cook or warm food after a day at work? And in the mornings did she make her porridge? Did she have a fridge? The fridge had been Stella's, which she moved to her house in Church Street.

I must have stopped listening at some stage, as it became too much to endure. I was always anxious about everybody's safety,

especially Dor's in Lansdowne. When I was at school in Claremont, I fretted about Mavie's safety in Woodlands. I fretted about
everybody's safety to saturation point. After which there was
nothing, just feeling numb and tired all the time.

How does one get through a lifetime of depression when it was
something no one wanted to acknowledge they had? You just went
on, in the hope that someday it would all be alright and the met-
aphorical worms would depart from the fruit trees without need-
ing to trim or spray with insecticides.

Some of the neighbours, whose families had bought land at the
same time as Great-grandpa Joe had, stayed on in their homes
because the owner or the inherited title-deed owner was still
alive. They refused to sell: the Cascar, Faulman, Stevens and
Lewis families, among others. Also the owners of Queen Bess,
Hamid's, Niefies, Lee-Pan and the shops down the side streets,
they stayed on right until apartheid devoured itself. These days
most of the shops are owned by Asian or East African migrants
and are completely lacking in the charm those old shops with
their many hidden surprises had.

In 1980, after six decades of being the McBain family home, the
property was sold for something like R13 000 to developers lined
up by the government officials. It was a quarter of the market
value of what the properties were worth then (it cost R10 000 to
buy a house on a single erf in the area that year). The lawyer
took about R6 000, supposedly for death duties. He was struck
off the roll for dodgy dealings a few years later. The rest was
divided between Grandpa Jack's widow Miss Lizzie and six of
the siblings.

Thus, ended Great-grandpa Joe's dream.

Before Dor moved to stay with Stella and Meneer Wilfie on the-other-side-of-the-line Lansdowne, sixty years of family history had to be cleared out of the house at 10 Heatherley Road, Lansdowne, and the land that surrounded it.

The dining room furniture and the 1937 Humber went to Uncle Joey's house, two sideboards went to Stella, and the Jewel stove went to Uncle Johnny's house in Bridgetown. Most of the other pieces of furniture were given away. Mavie took some crockery. She had a fully furnished house and didn't want anything.

Crockery was divided up. Metal from the garage was sold. The rest of the building paraphernalia that they found in the ceiling – long past its prime – the cousins ditched down the well (the pump had been sold too). Great-grandpa Joe's Bible, all the family documents and all the photos from the late 1800s onwards went to Stella's house in Church Street. She and Dor were the keepers of the records.

For about a year, Dor went to work every day at the surgery on the corner of Lansdowne Road and Hanbury Avenue and watched the bulldozers through the dispensary window, levelling her life. In its place, four identical houses for white people soon rose out of the ground.

Dor loved that garden, all gardens, all of nature, to grow plants, to dig into the soil, to watch life grow, to behold flowers and to make art from the blooms, all to the glory of God. If she was around today, I would share Kahlil Gibran's quote with her: 'Sadness is but a wall between two gardens.'

More endings were to follow.

In the Woodlands home, hearth and nuclear family never worked out for my parents and me. Ivan had always had what is best described in Afrikaans as *'n lang oog vir die vroumense,* or better still, he was a *meireboef.* In Mitchells Plain, far away from our known past and the judging eyes of the uppities and older relatives, he soon took up with a mistress. Opportunity presented itself in a sultry Catholic widow from around the corner on Ajax Way.

It was scandalous and a great big *bladdie* embarrassment. Just four years after the move to our new house and a few months after Granny Davids had died in 1981, Ivan filed for divorce. He perjured himself in legal documents before the court, thereby allowing Mavie the can't-ever-get-divorced Catholic to win a settlement. This stopped the sale of the Woodlands property and bound him in knots until he died a decade later.

Mavie fought the fight on principle and with her signature sense of humour. She was absolutely right not to roll over and play dead as many, especially the priests, wanted her to do. She had her honour to save. For a short while, she did worry about not being able to receive communion at church in Lentegeur, but Father Donaghy ran intervention and called the Chancery at St Mary's Cathedral. They declared that she could still receive communion because she had not been at fault nor had she filed for the divorce.

After the divorce, family and friends asked Mavie if she would revert to her maiden name. She immediately dismissed the question with a pithy comment. 'I like the anonymity of the surname,' she told them. This despite the fact that it had never gone well with her name – it was a source of amusement for the nursing sisters and patients when 'Mavis Davids' was called at the day hospital. But Mavie said it was better than her maiden name because McBain stuck out like a sore thumb.

Ivan's family surname had always been a great mystery to my male cousins who love the drama of the mysterious. I had a theory about it though. I figured that the original slave had been called David because on a beach somewhere in Southeast Asia he threw stones at the big red giants that wanted to catch him and take him away from his doe-eyed mistresses. I never dared utter this theory to my uncles or cousins. I would have been on the receiving end of some verbal stone-throwing, I have no doubt.

Neither Ivan nor Mavie could afford their long legal battle and it took them years to pay off the costs individually. From that, I learnt valuable lessons on how not to be, who not to be with, and what to avoid in life to survive. My list of prejudices grew by leaps and bounds.

Although a good many years of other lives were lived wherever the family members landed, there was no getting away from the fact that home was no longer Heatherley Road. Did we all die at the moment we accepted the removal? Who knows?

In terms of grieving, each handled it according to his or her character. And perhaps uprootedness left us all a little selfish – always looking inward, looking back – and nobody talked about how they actually felt, not realising that others were as emotionally frail. Always the empty reassurances that the new house was 'nicer', that it was 'our own', that 'the roof doesn't leak'. No one ever said 'it's to hell and gone far'. No one considered themselves to be maladjusted.

As a teenager, I didn't understand what it meant to grieve, how necessary it is to go through all the grieving stages. It was such an intense emotional climate. I just didn't know how to react to anything. When you're in an all-new environment with new people and you don't know where they came from or who they're connected to and how to act around them, it's hard. Sometimes, when my meagre coping skills ran out, I exploded in rage.

I certainly didn't understand what the adults were going through. I didn't know about depression or the other consequences of living in stressful conditions for prolonged periods. And I didn't know that I was suffering from it too – and had been for a long time.

After matric, for eight years, I led an unsettled life; drifting between two warehouse jobs, seven months studying social science at UWC and about eight months as a student nurse until my unresolved past led me into journalism.

From my mid-twenties onwards, for about six years, I had a ringside view of the dying days of apartheid, seeing its many faces all at once. I stood on the edges of black fury vs. white fury. I watched and made notes and was appalled. How to make sense of *that* mêlée?

I couldn't turn away. I had to see what would happen to this entity called apartheid that had been humming away ominously all my life, this monster that I had seen systematically destroy homes and lives and people's history, including my own family's, long before I had the capacity to understand what was happening right before my eyes.

When I first became a newspaper reporter, I crossed boundaries, most of which I did not even know existed. I went to places I ordinarily would not have visited, like the squatter camps or the posh hotels and super-rich mountainside suburbs or the bastions of Afrikanerdom: Stellenbosch University, the northern suburbs' town council meetings, a National Party meeting in Clanwillian – even a press conference of the Afrikaner Weerstandsbeweging (the AWB), a white supremacist neo-nazi outfit. I spoke to people I would never have spoken to before, scribbling down their incredible stories.

I climbed hills and the mountain as I had done in my growing up years, but some of those peaks were in areas that had been reserved for whites – rich whites, not like the whites who'd been our neighbours or my own reclassified family. I went to beaches that had been whites-only beaches to report on sports events or to write pretty stories about what holidaymakers were up to, all while other parts of the city and country were burning.

I sat at the magistrates' courts and the Supreme Court – now the Cape High Court – and listened to the many acts of cruelty people inflicted on other people. I saw rapists, murderers, drug dealers, brothel owners, terrorists and paedophiles. I went to Paarl, Brown's Farm, Hout Bay, Sites B and C and Green Point in Khayelitsha. Many times it was to witness the same face of apartheid that I had seen for most of my childhood and teen years – the face that bulldozed homes and removed people as though they were rubbish.

As my professional experience grew, I was sent on assignments deep in the battle zones where protest marches turned violent. There would be stone-throwing. Boulders, rubble and burning tyres barricading roads. Riot police would beat and chase, shoot teargas canisters or birdshot, or live ammunition meant to kill.

I asked questions on all sides of the conflict, and people spoke to me because of my job. And yet it was a strange time of many stories left untold and many impressions left undeciphered because of the crippling restrictions placed on the media in the 1980s and 1990s, especially during the state of emergency.

The combatants did not speak the same languages. The only language they had in common was anger. And if they spoke the same language, it was in key words, clichés that came paired with charm offensives, propaganda or rhetoric, and most times all of it together.

It was exhausting listening to the many organisations' representatives talking and talking and saying nothing at all. And what a battle it was to translate those angry sounds into good English for a family newspaper.

Maybe the most revealing thing of all was in the aftermath of violent confrontation, when all combatants had spent their forces, how the battlefield – usually a road or a bridge – was littered with empty shells, sticks, stones, clothing items and shoes lost in flight. After all the chaos and noise, all that was left was an overwhelming sense of absence and silence. A deafening silence. In my mind, it became a metaphor for the apartheid era's lingering death.

It was much like the deafening silence of the forced removals – the silence that descended when all that was left of my home, and other people's homes throughout the country, was the land on which a beloved house had once stood.

After I had done my time on apartheid's deathwatch, the tediousness of the work got to me and I walked away. At that time, in 1992, no one knew what to expect. More of that endless worry and uncertainty which I was more than familiar with after 31 years of my life spent at apartheid's beck and call.

The following year, one wintry June day shortly before my 32nd birthday, I stood facing the ocean with a cardboard box in my hands. I had to empty the contents into the grey-green waves of False Bay, off the Kalk Bay sea wall. A lone seagull cast a beady eye my way.

There we stood: Mavie, Cousin Lee-Lee with baby Lisa in her arms, Cousin Mark and me, looking at the box and knowing that a prayer had to be said over the contents before they were put to sea. The cousins joined us because they lived close by in Strandfontein.

Eventually, Mavie, the much-maligned ex-wife, said the Lord's Prayer and we were all satisfied, knowing full well that the contents, which used to be Ivan, were a wannabe-anything-but-not-Christian. He would surely have preferred a Buddhist mantra, but none of us had one.

I might have said, 'Abracadabra, Open Sesame', which was more his kind of line. Or better still, 'I must go down to the seas again, for the call of the running tide is a wild call and a clear call that may not be denied; / And all I ask is a windy day with the white clouds flying, And the flung spray and the blown spume, and the sea-gulls crying.'

Ivan never failed to recite the poem 'Sea Fever' by John Masefield on our tours of the Peninsula, especially just at that last rise when the road ended at the Strandfontein Point – now The Strandfontein Pavillion – and the spread of False Bay came into view. But rousing performances and I were an equation that just never came into being.

I decided to set Ivan off from Kalk Bay because that was where he'd pushed off from on his long-distance swims to Muizenberg, years before the increase in shark attacks and sightings in the bay. The last time he swam that route was a month before he died of heart failure at his desk at work at the age of 59.

And so I sat on the wall and emptied the contents – illegally – together with the flowers Mr Roberts the undertaker had given us. Within ten minutes the tide swept everything far out into the bay.

Much later I would count that aged sea wall at Kalk Bay as a beauty among many in the world that I had seen on my travels. It was a place to stand and to gaze out across the vast expanse of blue or grey or turquoise or azure or green, or a mixture of all the colours, to the mountains on the opposite coastline. The gaze became the point of departure from what was.

A year after Ivan, apartheid died in April 1994. It has yet to be buried completely.

Aunty Doreen, Ivan's eldest sister, who had loved Shakespeare and all things French, died in her seventies a month after her brother.

Dor died when she was 74 in 2002. Eight years later Stella, aged 78, and Mavie, aged 73, died less than a month apart – one at the start of 2010 World Cup and the other after the end of the tournament. Both of them had been ill for four years. Stella's husband Meneer Wilfie died five months before Dor.

Their days of duty to family, friends, foes and fakes had to end in brokenheartedness, even though they all strived through their individual pursuits never to end up that way.

My family's ties to Great-grandpa Joe's legacy had finally been severed, it felt to me.

Mavie and Stella at 80 Church Street, Lansdowne, Stella's house, about three months before they died, 2010.

In my words

My doodle of the house.

THAT WAS LONG AGO.

It was inevitable that the Carole King song 'So far away' was on my mind as I remembered the past, especially the chorus: 'So far away, doesn't anybody stay in one place anymore / It would be so fine to see your face at my door / Doesn't help to know you're just time away'.

I went back to Lansdowne on 24 December 2018.

On the bus ride from Claremont, I had built up an expectation that the stumps of the oak trees on Heatherley Road and the huge Norfolk pine on Dale Street would still be there and I would be able to take photos. I was imagining taking photos of the age rings. The stumps had still been there in March 2018, the last time I had been at Dr Emdin's surgery on the corner of Hanbury Avenue and Lansdowne Road (renamed Imam Haron Road in 2012).

As the bus passed Heatherley Road, I saw that the stumps were gone. Ditto on Dale Street. Where they had been, the ground had been levelled and paved over, all neat and uniform. Forlorn and choked up, coughing from the ash of memory, I stood at the narrow windows in front of the surgery, more or less in the same spot where Dor would have stood, gazing down Dale Street and seeing the bulldozers demolish our old home. I felt weighed down by tremendous sadness.

The neatly paved frontages of the houses were a far cry from what had been there: any crazy paving, slate, brick and concrete, or whatever piece of found terracotta or clay fragment or beautifully formed sandstone had attracted Great-grandpa Joe's eclectic tastes. A collection he'd started some 99 years earlier when Lansdowne was transitioning from being farmland and wetland to a residential area.

The charm, the imagination and art of unbridled nature, the quirky building style were stuck in the past in my mind. They would never return.

In February 2019, I learnt that all the family records and photographs and Great-grandpa Joe's Bible were no more. Stella had bequeathed these to Joline, my eldest cousin, but it was not handed over to her. The house had been left to Meneer Wilfie's sister Cecelia who had looked after Stella during her lingering illness. After Stella died in 2010, Cecelia cleaned away the past. She threw away the Bible 'because the pages were loose and crumbly'. The Word of God discarded in a charcoal-coloured City of Cape Town wheelie bin. Old rubbish.

She'd burnt the photos 'because I did not know the people in them'. The photos included Meneer Wilfie's brilliant record of the destruction of District Six, which his Vista High colleagues had asked Stella to donate to the District Six Museum after he died.

'*Ou goed,*' Cecelia said.

Old things.

Claremont, August 2019

Glossary

Chommie: friend

Bis: being a busybody

Bioscope: cinema

Hoekom moet jy alles bederf?: Why must you spoil everything?

Dikbek: surly, cross

Moerkoffie: brewed coffee

'Wat? Wat loer jy?': 'What? What are you looking at?'

Café: coffee

Pasteis de nata: Portuguese egg custard tartlets

Goose: girlfriend

Amigo: friend

Meneer: mister. Meneer is used to show respect to a teacher.

Halwe naartjies (nasies): half nations, mixed nations

Ou: guy, chap, boyfriend

Trek die siel uit: provoke the soul through teasing or taunting

Perlemoen: abalone

Konfyt: fruit preserve

Ouvrou-onder-die-kombers: old woman under a blanket. Usually refers to left-over meat coated in a batter and fried, or meatballs wrapped in cabbage leaves.

Smoortjies: a concoction of lunch meat, eggs, polony or smoked fish made into a stew or sauce from onions, tomatoes, potatoes, peppers, mushrooms, salt and pepper and a little sugar. It takes no more than ten to fifteen minutes to cook until the various flavours are blended. Usually eaten with bread or rice.

Bakkie: bowl

Bredie: stew

Frikkadels: meatballs

Brood-in-die-pot: bread browned in the pot

Lekker: nice

Kreef: crayfish

Doek: a cloth

Doekpoeding: steamed pudding

Kuite: fish eggs formed into the appearance of sausages and usually fried in oil.
   It is white on the inside and browned on the outside.

Kaiings: animal tail fat cooked until crisp, eaten as a snack

Skel: to scold

Laaities: young children, lightweights

Bliksem: to beat up

Kleinniggie: second cousin, daughter of a cousin

Kerriehol: curry bum

Bladdie: slang for bloody

Skelm: thief

Padkos: picnic food, literally 'road food'

Plak: stick or glue down

Skrik: a fright

Sub A and Sub B: Grades 1 and 2

Standards: grades

Kens: feeble-minded

En plein: to paint outside

Oupa: grandpa

Verkrampte: conservative or uptight

Skandelik: scandalous

Seun: son

Braaivleis: barbecue

Vygies: a veld flower that opens in the sun and closes at night

Stoep: a veranda

Kruisement: an indigenous medicinal herb

Buchu: an indigenous medicinal herb

Bokkoms: dried salted fish

Die Stem: The Call of South Africa – South African anthem during the apartheid era. In democratic South Africa is has been blended with Nkosi Sikele i'Africa (God Bless Africa) to form a hybrid anthem.

Wielie Walie: Afrikaans children's variety programme which aired on television for decades

Koorliedjies and moppies: Cape Malay choir songs and a cappella choruses

Die Ou Pastorie: residence of the minister of the Dutch Reformed Church

Suikerbrood: sugar bread

Soetkoekies: sweet biscuits usually made with a hint of ginger and all-spice

Juffrou: Miss, juffrou is used to show respect to a teacher

'n Lang oog vir die vroumense: an eye for the ladies, a roving eye, always positioning himself for a flirtation or a fling

Meireboef: ladies' man

Volksies: Volkswagen Beetles

Goema: goema is the beat played on the hand drum of the same name, traditionally played by the Cape Minstrels

Hare: hair

Ghoemahare: candy floss

Pennetjies: straight hair

Fokoff, voetsak: swear words meaning go away

Fokkol: nothing

Ou goed: old things

Acknowledgements

I HAVE MANY PEOPLE to thank who gave me endless helping hands through some extremely harsh years. I would have to write another book with just your names. So thank you.

For those who helped me during the year of writing this book, I will always appreciate what you did. A big, big thank you to:

- Andrea Weiss from WWF, NB Publishers' Erika Oosthuysen, head of non-fiction, and Kwela Books non-fiction publisher Na'eemah Masoet, who collectively pushed me off the wall into a sea of memories – and words and into this book;
- The Jakes Gerwel Foundation Writers Mentorship Project, JGF Executive Director Theo Kemp and mentor and editor Suzette Kotzé-Myburgh, and everybody else who made the time spent in mentorship at Paulet House (The Writer's House) in Somerset East so great: Mentor/Editor Francois Bloemhof and fellow mentees Engela Ovies, Shana Fife and Sharon Mogoaneng, and Michelle van Niekerk and Janet Telian for memorable meals, Paulet House manager Beneatha Adams and Kouga Shuttles driver Justin Woolls for safe travels
- Thank you for your support that came in many forms: Esmê Davids and family in Elfindale; Jo Firfirey and family in Grassy Park; Olive Adams and family in New Zealand; USA/Muizenberg friends Dirk and Elizabeth Wood, Gloria and

James Young and Chris and Tre Kitson; Dr Les Emdin; Greg Davids and staff at Urban Soul for work on the MCBB jazz project; Eugene du Plessis and staff at SA Mobile Drug Testing for freelance work; Jean Benn, Mervyn Blythe, Joan Kruger, Yolanda Wilson, Dennis Adams, Cathy and Willie Oliver, Lynne and Sian Wong and many neighbours in Claremont for their care and kindness. Many thanks to Sisanda Nkoala for transcription and translation work; homegrown Clyde Rix who spent four years evoking memory of the sights, sounds and tastes of home turf and church; Genevieve Callaghan for being a patron of my artwork, and to Karin Schimke for editing this offering;

– Also to Facebook friends, many of them top Cape Town newspaper and magazine editors, journalists, columnists and authors who encouraged me when I first made posts of my memories. Thank you! Thank you! Thank you, one and all, for the support you have given.

BRONWYN DAVIDS was born at 10 Heatherley Road, Lansdowne and lived there until the age of fifteen. She attended St Ignatius Primary School and Livingstone High School in Claremont. In 1976 she moved with her parents to Woodlands, Mitchells Plain at the inception of the new "city for coloureds".

After years of drifting between several courses of study and jobs, she studied for a National Diploma in Journalism at Peninsula Technikon, Bellville and graduated in 1989. During the dying days of apartheid, from 1988 to 1992, she was a reporter at *The Argus* and *Cape Times*.

Highlights from her career included assignments with four Nobel Peace Prize laureates, Mother Teresa of Calcutta during her visit to Cape Town, a road trip to the Boland with Nelson Mandela just after his release from prison, and attending press conferences with former President FW De Klerk at Tuynhuys and Anglican Archbishop Desmond Tutu at St George's Cathedral.

After leaving newspapers she travelled extensively to twenty countries on six continents. She then spent years painting and working at a series of jobs outside of journalism. In 2016 she returned to work at Newspaper House as a general news journalist at the *Cape Times*, *Cape Argus* and *Weekend Argus*, until January 2018. She freelances at present.